MUSIC OF THE SPHERES

Connecting to the Great Universal Consciousness and to ALL THAT IS through the music of Irish composer/pianist Pat McCourt

By Eileen McCourt

Music of the Spheres: Connecting to the Great Universal Consciousness and to ALL THAT IS through the music of Irish composer/pianist Pat McCourt

This book was first published in Great Britain in paperback during June 2018.

The moral right of Eileen McCourt is to be identified as the author of this work and has been asserted by her in accordance with the Copyright, Designs and Patents Act of 1988.

All rights are reserved and no part of this book may be produced or utilized in any format, or by any means, electronic or mechanical, including photocopying, recording or by any information storage or retrieval system, without prior permission in writing from the publishers - Coast & Country/Ads2life. ads2life@btinternet.com

All rights reserved.

ISBN-13: 978-1983223808

Copyright © June 2018 Eileen McCourt

CONTENTS

Page

About the author	i
Acknowledgements	ix
Review	x
Foreword	xiii
Chapter 1: The Music of the Spheres	1
Chapter 2: The Ancient Mystery Schools and Teachings	4
Chapter 3: Body and Soul	11
Chapter 4: What we are	36
Chapter 5: The One Great Universal Consciousness	40
Chapter 6: The Soul and the Higher Self	46
Chapter 7: Beyond our five physical senses	49
Chapter 8: Holding us all together – The interconnectedness of all things	58
Chapter 9: Getting into the Zone – raising our spiritual vibration	62
Chapter 10: Cymatics, harmonious resonance and the Ancients	67
Chapter 11: Music and the body and soul	81
Chapter 12: The Musicality and Spirituality of William Butler Yeats	89
Chapter 13: The Musicality and Spirituality of William Percy French	103
CONCLUSION: "If Music be the food of love, play on!"	119
Other Books by Eileen McCourt	125

ABOUT THE AUTHOR

Eileen McCourt is a retired school teacher of English and History with a Master's degree in History from University College Dublin.

She is also a Reiki Grand Master teacher and practitioner, having qualified in Ireland, England and Spain, and has introduced many of the newer modalities of Reiki healing energy into Ireland for the first time, from Spain and England. Eileen has qualified in England through the Lynda Bourne School of Enlightenment, and in Spain through the Spanish Federation of Reiki with Alessandra Rossin, Bienstar, Santa Eulalia, Ibiza.

Regular workshops and healing sessions are held in Elysium Wellness, Newry, County Down; New Moon Holistics N.I. Carrickfergus, County Antrim; Angel Times Limerick; Spirit 3 Ballinasloe County Galway; Sacred Space Newbridge County Kildare; Celtic School of Sound Healing Swords County Dublin and Holistic Harmony Omagh County Tyrone, where Eileen teaches all of the following to both practitioner and teacher levels:

- **Tibetan Usui Reiki levels 1, 2, 3, 4 and Grand Master**
- **Tera-Mai Reiki Seichem**
- **Okuna Reiki (Atlantean and Lemurian)**
- **Reiki Karuna (Indian)**
- **Rahanni Celestial Healing**
- **Fire Spirit Reiki (Christ Consciousness and Holy Spirit)**
- **Mother Mary Reiki**

- Mary Magdalene Reiki
- Archangels Reiki
- Archangel Ascended Master Reiki
- Violet Flame Reiki
- Lemurian Crystal Reiki
- Golden Eagle Reiki (Native North American Indian)
- Golden Chalice Reiki
- Golden Rainbow Ray Reiki
- Goddesses of Light Reiki
- Unicorn Reiki
- Pegasus Reiki
- Elementals Reiki
- Dragon Reiki
- Dolphin Reiki
- Pyramid of Goddess Isis Reiki
- Magnified Healing of the God Most High of the Universe
- Psychic Surgery

This is Eileen's 15th book.

Previous publications include:

- **'Living the Magic'**, published in December 2014
- **'This Great Awakening'**, September 2015
- **'Spirit Calling! Are You Listening?'**, January 2016
- **'Working With Spirit: A World of Healing'**, January 2016
- **'Life's But A Game! Go With The Flow!'**, March 2016
- **'Rainbows, Angels and Unicorns!'**, April 2016
- **'........And That's The Gospel Truth!'**, September 2016
- **'The Almost Immaculate Deception! The Greatest Scam in History?'**, September 2016
- **'Are Ye Not Gods?' The true inner meanings of Jesus' teachings and messages'**, March 2017
- **'Jesus Lost and Found'**, July 2017
- **'Behind Every Great Man........ Mary Magdalene Twin Flame of Jesus'**, July 2017
- **'Out of the Mind and into the Heart: Our Spiritual Journey with Mary Magdalene'**, August 2017
- **'Divinely Designed: The Oneness of the Totality of ALL THAT IS'**, January 2018
- **' Resurrection or Resuscitation?: What Really Happened in That Tomb?'**, May 2018

Eileen has also recorded 6 guided meditation CDs with her brother, pianist Pat McCourt:

- *'Celestial Healing'*
- *'Celestial Presence'*
- *'Cleansing, energising and balancing the Chakras'*
- *'Ethereal Spirit'*
- *'Open the Door to Archangel Michael'*
- *'Healing with Archangel Raphael'*

All publications are available from Amazon online and all publications and CDs are in Angel and Holistic centres around the country, as specified on website.

Website: www.celestialhealing8.co.uk

Eileen is currently working on her 16th book 'Chakras, Crystals and Colours - a child's second Spiritual book', which is the sequel to 'Rainbows, Angels and Unicorns'.

ACKNOWLEDGEMENTS

I wish to thank, yet again, my publishers, Don Hale OBE and Dr. Steve Green for their patience, advice and input.

And my sincere thanks, yet again, to all who have been constantly supporting and encouraging me in my work. You all know who you are!

Sincere and heart-felt appreciation to all of you who are buying my books and CDs and for your kind comments.

Thank you to all who attend my workshops and courses, and to all who have taken the time to write reviews for me, both in my books and on Amazon. You are greatly appreciated!

Special thanks to Cheryl McWilliams for helping me to interpret the various sounds of the planets, especially the sound of the moon, which is like bees humming around the Queen Bee. Cheryl's business is Mother Bee, natural products mostly for animals but also for us. So if anyone can recognise the sound of bees, it is Cheryl! She is based in Benburb, County Tyrone, Northern Ireland. (www.motherbeeonline.co.uk)

Special thanks too, to Declan Quigley, Shamanic practitioner, teacher, writer and founder of Anam Nasca Shamanism Ireland, for his contribution, Chapter 10 in this book. Declan runs workshops, training seminars and healing clinics throughout Ireland and beyond. (anamnasca@gmail.com)

And of course, thank you to my brother Pat McCourt, for the pleasure and joy he brings to people with his music, and without whom this book would not possibly have materialised.

Finally, as always, I give thanks for all the wonderful blessings that are constantly being bestowed upon us in this wonderful, loving, abundant Universe.

Namaste!

Eileen McCourt

7th July 2018

REVIEW

'Music of the Spheres' is a one-off book that deals with a unique subject matter very rarely written about, but nevertheless very prevalent in this modern society.

The book apprises us all to the degree to which we are connected to the universe via the virtuosity of music and vibration. We are enlightened by the fact that we do not just emit sounds through our vocal chords, but we emit multiple sound vibrations that connect us to every single thing in our universe.

The author gives us extremely detailed, informative descriptions as to how this occurs by using her brother, the composer and pianist Pat McCourt as the perfect example of how we can all attain musical vibratory Oneness.

Enlighteningly superb, descriptively superlative, what an inspired author is Eileen McCourt!

Clare Bowman, Spiritual Historian

FOREWORD

Growing up as children, our home was always filled with the sound of my young brother Pat playing the piano. We had, literally, constant in-house entertainment. He began his musical career at the tender young age of four. He would just sit there at the piano, his little legs and feet not even touching the floor or able to reach the pedals. As children do, we just took it all for granted. That was Pat and that was just what Pat did.

Pat's talent was a source of pride to both our parents of course, and rightly so. Our father delighted in the exceptional skills of his one and only son, steadfast in his encouragement, nourishing and feeding him a diet of William Percy French and Stephen Foster among others, and what we would now call '*golden oldies*', dancing about the place and singing, or trying to sing in time to Pat's music. He himself could only manage one finger of his right hand on the piano, nothing at all with his left, but he usually managed to hit the right note with that one finger. He was an avid reader, with books all over the place, and he would engross himself in his reading. But many a time I saw him slowly lower the book and prick up his ears as Pat began to play in a distant room, the music permeating into every nook and corner. And then, unable to contain himself, he would put the book aside, get up from his chair and make his way to the source of the music.

Yes, Pat was naturally gifted. Music was in both sides of the family, so as they say, he didn't pick it up off the street! But even with that, Pat seemed to have been endowed with more than his fair share of talent. I must have been behind the door when that talent was being given out, and there was Pat, both little hands outstretched, ready to receive my share as well as his own!

His talent, of course has nothing to do with the fact that Pat came into this world feet first, nor the fact that he continues to flaunt convention in his own free-Spirited way. The Universe looks after him, he goes with the flow, and Spirit flows through him in his musical compositions.

The years pass, and as naturally happens, we all go on our own separate journey of life. But looking back now, I always knew there was something going on when Pat was playing the piano. There was some sort of connection being made between him and something else. Something else outside of himself in which he was completely immersed. He was in another world, the music just flowing through him, gushing like water through a fountain. That piano that I thought back then was merely a piece of wood just came alive under him, as his fingers deftly and rapidly traversed along the keyboard. I did not understand what it was, nor did I think very much about it at that time. As I said, that was Pat and that was just what Pat did. But when I heard other people play the piano, either in this country or in foreign places, I knew there was something very different. It was not so much what he played, as how he played it. It was not just what I always called the 'twiddly bits' of his own that he incorporated into everything he played. He was not just playing notes on a piano, like reading from a script. He was in a different zone, beyond human contact, carried along in something which I at that time just did not understand. Was it some sort of escape or release mechanism for dealing with every day life? Or was it something way beyond that?

It was only much later in my life, when I became a Reiki practitioner in fact, that I finally realised what it was all about. As I was receiving my attunement to the Reiki symbols, I had my very first spiritual experience, and to say that I was blown away by it all there and then just as I was actually being attuned, is far from an exaggeration. The overwhelming emotion that engulfed me, the most wonderful and blissful feeling of what I can only describe as total and unconditional love that swamped me, surrounding me and enfolding me in something outside of this earthly plane. For just then, at that moment in time, when time itself stopped for me, I touched my own soul for the very first time.

And I knew then what I had been wondering about so many times before. I now knew what was happening when my brother Pat played the piano. He was connecting with his own soul! After all, he was not nick-named *'Angel fingers'* at school for nothing! And playing the grand organ in Saint Patrick's Cathedral in Armagh at only twelve years of age! His fingers took on a life of their own, especially those attached to his left hand!

As I continued on my spiritual path, incorporating more and more Reiki practices into my life, and introducing many of the newer modalities of higher celestial energies into Ireland for the first time, from Spain and England, I strongly felt my deepening connection to **Spirit**, to **All That Is.** Then when my books began to materialise, all coming in rapid succession one after the other, I experienced for myself what it is to be **'in-spired'** to be **'in Spirit',** to go with that ' **'Inspiration'** as it flowed through me.

That **'inspiration',** that **'creative'** part of a person, that process that produces a musical composition or a great work of art, is **receptive and not active.** One does not just sit down and start to think up a musical composition, a poem, a piece of sculpture or a piece of art.

One does not compose or create on demand or on purpose or according to dictates. It just does not work that way! It just comes! All one has to do is *just be* and let the creativity flow. And from where is it flowing? From the **Great Universal God Consciousness**. From the higher echelons, beyond our physical plane, from the higher vibrational frequencies.

And with all my work with the higher celestial energies, I have come to know and experience other energy vibrational frequencies, and to deeply sense and feel the other multi-dimensional vibrational energies that constantly surround us on all sides, swirling and dancing and inter-connecting with us on so many levels. And I now know that piano that Pat played was not just a piece of wood, but a form of life, a *consciousness* emanating from its tree origins, a *consciousness* that was responding to Pat's soul, pulsating and throbbing with life, as he poured his essence into it, connecting with the **Music of the Spheres**, connecting with the **Great Universal God Energy,** the **Great Universal God Consciousness,** which runs through all things and outside of which nothing, no person or no form of life can have any existence. Pat **became** the music, he **was** the music, in total harmony with the **Music of the Spheres, 'Musica Universalis',** which is part of the core being of our essence.

According to some of the great philosophers and thinkers, such as Pythagoras, Aristotle and Plato, there is a mathematical relationship between all the planets throughout the entirety of creation, and that harmonious connection, that mathematical, ordered and proportionately structured connection between the earth, the sun, the moon and all the other planets was the origin of the perfect harmony of our world, our Planet Earth. Pythagoras taught, in a theory that became known as the **Music of the Spheres**, that all the planets in movement, as they rotate, create a melody of sound, a vibration, a perfect harmonious note that resonates throughout the entirety of creation. And that musical vibration of all the planets affects us here on earth. Our quality of life here on earth is indeed influenced by this vibration of the planets and the universe.

So that is what this book is about. Connecting to **Spirit,** to **All That Is,** to the **Music of the Spheres.** And how, through the music and the musical compositions of Pat McCourt, we too can be connected to the **Music of the Spheres**, connected to **All That Is** as we listen to him play. As he plays, he is making that divine connection, and as we listen, we are making that divine connection too, through Pat, who has, through his playing, raised our spiritual vibration sufficiently to enable us to make that connection. Through becoming **One** with him, we then become **One** with the **Great Universal God Energy**, the **Great Universal Consciousness,** thus feeling the love of the Creator.

Of course we can reach a higher state of consciousness through various practices such as meditation or yoga or even through some trance-inducing drugs! But music is played in all holistic therapy rooms throughout the world, in waiting rooms, on public transport, everywhere! And have you ever wondered why? Because of the effect it has on us! As **William Percy French** said, **'Music held me in its magic spell'.**

And if music is indeed the magic spell, then those who compose the music are the magicians. They wield the power. The power to transport us above this earthly dimension. The power to enable us to feel the **Oneness of all Creation**, and to experience the profound, unlimited, unconditional love of the Creator.

And **Pat McCourt** is one such magician! As was **William Percy French** before him, William Percy French who has secured a place in our hearts forever with his songs, his melodies and his poetry! As was also **William Butler Yeats**, with the musicality of his poetry. Yes, music runs through everything, for as we shall see through the chapters of this book, music is a vibration, just as we all are. And Pat McCourt has indeed, through his own captivating compositions, put many of William Butler Yeats' works as well as some of William Percy French's poems to music!

To watch and to listen to Pat play is to experience for one's self the symphony of the **Music of the Spheres**. As Pat plays, he moves constantly through the octaves, his left hand not just accompanying his right hand, but taking on a life of its own. His left hand dominates his right hand, now it submits, all in a swirling mass of vibrational energy, all in a combination of harmonious chords delightful to the ear. Sheer genius!

Such talent is a natural endowment, maybe even rare. It cannot be learned through a series of classes, no matter how experienced the teacher. And there is often indeed a wide discrepancy between musical interest and musical talent. Many of those people to whom music is of vital importance are unable to express themselves through any particular instrument or ability to sing. Many music enthusiasts often moan about the fact that their lack of musical prowess is their greatest disappointment in life. And many more who have mastered a particular musical instrument are merely playing notes, objectively observing from a distance as their fingers do the talking. It takes talent to play or to compose with Soul.

And such talent has been gifted to be shared with others. And that is what Pat does. It has never been a money-making exercise in his life, nor has he ever sought fame. He shares his natural gift, bringing joy and pleasure to others.

Music is indeed a vibrational gateway, a gateway into a higher, expanded state of consciousness. As Pat moves beyond his physical realm, he becomes **One** with the universe, taking us with him. And that is the point at which we begin to feel our own spiritual vibration. That is the point at which we make our own connection with **Source**, with **All That Is,** with the **Great Universal God Consciousness**.

As I said before, that is Pat and that is just what Pat does.

CHAPTER 1:

The Music of the Spheres

It is surely ironic that in this, the 21st century, where we consider ourselves to be living in a very advanced world, and a very scientifically advanced world at that, that only now is science catching up with the teachings and theories of the ancients!

The ancients who had no technology such as we have, no machines, no electricity or power such as we have! How could it possibly be that those ancients were propounding scientific theories that only recently, our modern day scientists have been able to verify?

The notion or idea that the entire cosmos is a sublimely harmonious system, guided and directed by a Supreme Intelligence, omnipresent, omniscient and omnipotent, and that man has an eternal and preordained role in that system runs through Western civilization. And it is not a new idea!

It was Pythagoras who first propounded not only a scientific notion of the universe but also the notion of a musical universe. Pythagoras, who influenced Aristotle, Plato and through them, Western philosophy.

And Pythagoras lived 500 years before the time of Jesus!

500 years before Jesus! Difficult it certainly may be for us to get our heads around that!

But yes, Pythagoras lived 570 to 495 B.C.E.

We usually think of Pythagoras as the great mathematician that he was, the father and founder of modern mathematics. But that was not all he was! Nor was he indeed just a thinker and philosopher! And yes, while he was indeed the first to propound a scientific view of the cosmos, he was also a mystic who advocated a certain way of life. In fact, his way of life was the way of life lived by the ancient Essenes, that secretive sect of Judaism, living in Jewish Palestine before and during the time of Jesus, with branches known as Nazoreans and Ebionites, and in Egypt as Therapeutae, or healers. Was Jesus not known and referred to as '*Jesus the Nazorean*'? A term which has indeed been greatly misunderstood. Jesus the *Nazorean*, because he belonged to the *Nazoreans*, a branch of the Essenes, and not because he was, supposedly, from Nazareth.

The Essenes were a vast extensive network system of Brotherhood, extending through many centuries and many lands, during the last three centuries B.C.E and the first century C.E. They followed the teachings of ancient Persia, Egypt, India, Tibet, China and many other countries, transmitting all the knowledge in its most pure form. That esoteric knowledge was recorded in the Dead Sea Scrolls, found in caves in 1945 near the Dead Sea, where the Essene community of Qumran lived.

Their simple, pure, mainly agricultural, communal way of life, living on the shores of lakes and rivers, away from the cities and towns, and sharing equally in everything, meant that there were no poor or rich amongst them. They established their own economic system, based entirely on the Law, and were living proof that all man's food and material needs can be attained without struggle, through knowledge of the Law. They were proficient in prophecy, healing, astronomy, all passed down from the Ancient Mystery Schools of Persia and Egypt. They sent out teachers and healers from their communities to teach the inner, esoteric knowledge to those outside the Brotherhood, to those who were ready to listen.

And two of those who were sent out from the Essene community at Qumran to teach and heal were John the Baptist and of course, he who is known to us as Jesus, but who was known then as Yeshua.

Not long after the canonical gospels and the Acts of the Apostles were written, around 80 C.E. the Essenes were no longer in existence. Their teachings and doctrines had become heresy, their texts and writings being destroyed, just like all the other texts and writings that did not agree with the teachings of the early Roman Christian Church fathers. Those early Roman Christian Church fathers who were not in the least interested in Yeshua the man, but in Jesus the god-man, created in order to compete with all the other Roman gods of the day, all born of virgins, and all dying and resurrecting after three days.

So it was Pythagoras' teachings on which the whole Essene way of life was established. And from where did Pythagoras himself get his ideas and philosophies?

In Egypt, he studied geometry, where he was in fact the first foreigner to be initiated into the mysteries of the Ancient Egyptian religion. Then in Phoenicia he learned about numbers and proportions. His instructions in astronomy he received from the

Chaldeans, who were acknowledged by all antiquity to be the masters and experts of that science. One early biographer claims that while Pythagoras was in Chaldea, he studied with the famed Master Zoroaster, *'by whom he was purified from the pollutions of his past life, and taught about the things from which a virtuous man ought to be free. Likewise, he heard lectures about Nature and about the principles of wholes. It was from his stay among these foreigners that Pythagoras acquired the greatest part of his wisdom.'* (From *'Music of the Spheres'*, Jamie James)

Then he spent further time studying with the Magi, those wise men of ancient Persia, where he was taught other secrets concerning the course of life.

So from all his studying in the Ancient Mystery Schools, which we will look into further in the next chapter, and his time spent with those Ancient Masters, Pythagoras identified and propounded his theories about numbers, proportions and music. For Pythagoras and his followers, the Pythagoreans, numbers, proportions and music were all entirely congruent. The cosmos was music, music was number and everything in the cosmos was in proportion. The ancient Greek philosophers had referred to music as *'Sculptures in the air'*, the *'highest form of art;* and *'the one you cannot touch'*.

Yes, it was the Pythagoreans who first questioned the whole meaning and understanding of the universe, from what was it created, what was holding it all together, what was man, and what was man's place in the whole of creation.

Having made his wonderful discovery of the mathematical basis for the musical intervals, Pythagoras came to the conclusion that these mathematical truths must underlie the very principles of the universe. He recognised that

'..... they supposed the elements of numbers to be the elements of all things, and the whole heavens to be a musical scale and a number.' (Aristotle, 'On the Heavens')

For the purpose of this chapter, we are going to consider his theory that came to be known as **'The Music of the Spheres'**.

In 'The Music of the Spheres' Pythagoras first expounded the idea that the planets, as they constantly revolve on their orbital path must make sounds, and that being the case, these sounds would of necessity be musical and harmonious:

'The motion of bodies of that size must produce a noise, since on our earth the motion of bodies far inferior in size and speed of movement has that effect. Also, when the sun and the moon, they say, and all the stars, so great in number and in size, are moving with so rapid a motion, how could they not produce a sound immensely great? Starting from this argument, and the observation that their speeds, as measured by their distances, are in the same ratios as musical concordances, they assert that the sound given forth by the circular movement of the stars is a harmony.' (Aristotle, *'On The Heavens'*)

In his theory of 'The Music of the Spheres', Pythagoras claimed that he himself, due to his extremely acute sense of hearing, could actually hear the musical, harmonious sounds emitted by the planets as they rotated along their orbital path.

And we too, today can now hear those same sounds!

NASA has made them available to us through U-Tube! Now we can actually hear the sounds of the planets for ourselves, and know that Pythagoras' theory was indeed correct! We can now know that although space is a virtual vacuum, this does not mean there is no sound in space. Indeed, space is full of sound, carried by radio waves. NASA satellites and space stations have proved it. Indeed there is a '**Song of Planets**' to be clearly heard!

And how would one describe these sounds?

To me, Mercury sounds like a plane in the sky, or like a wind, increasing in intensity, then becoming like a throbbing sound, or a pulsing sound.

Venus emits a sound much like the melodious brimming of Tibetan bowls.

Uranus is like a high speed wind.

Saturn seems like a haunting sound, a bit like crying souls.

Jupiter is like church bells.

The Moon is like the sound of honey bees around the Queen bee.

The Sun is a series of pulsating sounds, all in rhythm.

Then the Earth, in contrast to them all, is definitely a heavier, much more dense vibrational sound, a bit like a car chugging along.

Earth definitely seems to me to be out of tune, like a radio station just not exactly tuned into that particular frequency.

And it makes me think, that if humans, as we know humans to be, ever come to inhabit any of these other planets, then will these planets be put out of balance too, in the same way that we humans have managed to put this beautiful earth out of balance?

So how can we sum up Pythagoras' contribution to what we call civilization? Certainly, Pythagorean ideas entered into mainstream Western thought and helped shape our culture. His teachings of a harmonious universe ordered and structured according to the 'Natural Order' or the 'Great Chain of Being', the continuum of matter, body, mind, soul and spirit, permeates Western thought, and is represented in all our educational institutions, theology, cosmology, literature, architecture, art, theology and science. All the thinkings of such men as Einstein, Newton, Aquinas, Kepler can all be traced back to the teachings of Pythagoras. And the writings of men like Aristotle and Plato were all deeply influenced by him.

'The 6th century scene evokes the image of an orchestra expectantly tuning up, each player absorbed in his own instrument only, deaf to the cauterwailings of the others. Then there is a dramatic silence, the conductor enters the stage, raps three times with his baton, and harmony emerges from the chaos. The master is Pythagoras of Samos, whose influence on the ideas, and thereby on the destiny, of the human race was probably greater than that of any single man before or after him.' (A musical metaphor used by Arthur Koestler, and quoted in *'Music of the Spheres'*, Jamie James, page 38)

Yes, the Pythagorean vision of the cosmos was indeed one of order and structure, everything divinely designed in proportion, everything mathematically structured and everything musically in a harmonious melody, all for the well-being of all creatures great and small.

And when we examine the various spiritual traditions on this planet, we see that they all have a commonality in their understanding that the universe was created through sound.

"And God said, 'Let there be light', the creation of sound preceded light. (The Old Testament: Genesis 1:3:)

'In the beginning was the Word'. (New Testament: John 1:1:)

From a scientific point of view, this manifestation of the universe through vibration is known as the *'Big Bang',* and sometimes as *'The Cosmic Hum'*.

As we have just seen, the ancients were aware that sound could make us feel via the Music of the Spheres. They were also aware that these sounds were an intrinsic part of the planetary and universal sounds beyond our physical hearing capacity, but still had an effect on the harmony of the earth and its inhabitants.

The great composers all sought some sort of intrinsic or spiritual guidance in composing great works of music and art. They invoked the 'Muses' for divine inspiration, tapping in somehow to the 'Cosmic Hum' or the 'Song of Planets', increasing their physical, Soul, and Higher Spirit levels of harmony. Mozart, Beethoven, Bach, Strauss and others were all able to connect to their muses and compose beautiful works.

Pat McCourt, a musician since four years of age, has composed a range of melodies which duplicates those greats who have gone before him. His musical compositions, as we will see in later chapters, allow us to attain a greater rise in our consciousness, uniting our Soul and universal Spirit. His music allows us to become One with ourselves and with the universe, thereby raising our consciousness, and with this increase in consciousness, we connect to our Higher Spirit and to the universe beyond.

To watch McCourt play, is indeed to be present at the symphony of the muses themselves. To listen to his music is to feel our own spiritual vibration. Whilst being in the presence of the Music of the Spheres, McCourt moves, plays and vibrates as One with the Spheres. He sees nothing around him because he is truly connected beyond his physical realm. His fingers move with an elegance which simulates the connection between his physical, his Soul and his Higher Spirit. He has become the music and when his connection is complete, he is at One with the universe.

Sound is simply a longitudinal pressure wave that vibrates backward and forwards in the same direction as the actual wave itself. All objects which vibrate, emit a sound wave outwards in all directions. Sound waves also have a lot of other scientific components, such as frequency, wave length and velocity.

As McCourt composes and plays music, the emanating sounds and melodies vibrate from the piano as sound waves. These then become attached to the natural vibrations of the universe in a resonant manner, increasing in harmony with both the composer and the universe. It is this resonant connection that evokes our emotive behaviour. We then want to become part of this resonant connection, and so we begin to tap our feet, move our body or start to dance.

We want to join with The Music of the Spheres. And McCourt is the medium through which we do this. We will see in the chapters throughout this book exactly how this does indeed happen!

But was the theory of the Music of the Spheres, which science has now proven to be accurate, just something that came into Pythagoras' head, something which just hit him as he strolled through the olive trees almost 2500 years ago? Hardly!

To find the answer, we need to take a look at the Ancient Mystery Schools and their teachings!

Chapter 2:

The Ancient Mystery Schools and Teachings

Many people today are completely unaware of the existence of the Ancient Mystery Schools as far back in history as over 4000 years before the time of Jesus, and continuing for several centuries after his death. History largely ignores these important establishments, in just the same way as the writers of all history deliberately decide what to include and what to leave out, depending on their own individual agenda.

But they definitely did exist, and as we saw in the previous chapter, it was in these Ancient Mystery Schools that Pythagoras studied and learned. And as I explained in a previous book, *'Jesus Lost and Found',* so too did Jesus.

Where was Jesus during those *'missing years'*, those years from he was twelve years old until he was thirty and beginning his ministry, those years unaccounted for in the gospels? Yes, Jesus was in foreign places studying and learning in the Ancient Mystery Schools, just like Pythagoras before him, and with the Druids in Gaul and Avalon. And what got him into so much trouble with the Jewish authorities, the Sanhedrin, the Pharisees and the Sadducees, so much trouble that he had to be got rid of, was the fact that he was teaching contrary to Jewish beliefs, what he had learned in the Ancient Mystery Schools. Indeed, his teachings were so contradictory to the beliefs of the Jewish people and so unacceptable, even so offensive to them that his life was in danger, so therefore he could not have gained all his knowledge, learning and healing skills in any place where the Jewish religion was established.

Based on deep philosophical thinkings, these Mystery Schools were developed in ancient times by the wise sages of many lands, supporting and guiding those who sought an alternative path to the shallow, artificial, destructive materialism of everyday living with its gross spiritual indifference, its superstitious ways, and its corrupt political and economic structures. They addressed the deeper meanings of existence, delving into the Spiritual world and into one's own inner Spiritual self for the answers to the deeper questions of life and death.

So what were these Mystery Schools? What were they teaching? How was this esoteric, inner knowledge passed on?

Today, most people are oblivious to the fact that all forms of life in the entire cosmos are connected. Many people simply exist on the material level, believing that this physical world is the centre of everything, the most important planet in existence. But there are others who know the truth. There are others who know that we here on Planet Earth are merely a small grain of sand in the entirety of all the universes in the totality of creation. There are those who know that the only difference between our small planet and all the other planets and universes is that we are all operating on different energy vibrational levels and that those different energy vibrational levels can be crossed by those who know how.

And there are those who know that we are all connected in the great universal Oneness of the entirety of creation. The microcosmic energy systems of the earth are interconnected with the vast macrocosmic systems of the stellar matrix, all held together by the most exquisite, the most intricate, the most ingenious of geometrical designs and mathematical equations, heaven-and-earth alignments and sonar sound vibrations of for example, the dolphins and whales.

But of course, all this knowledge is not available to the masses! Students in schools everywhere are taught mathematics and geometry, how to work out various mathematical and geometric equations, but they are not taught that it is mathematical equations and geometrical designs that hold entire creation together! Nor are they taught about the sonar sounds emitted by dolphins and whales and how they too hold creation together! Nor are they taught about all the subtle energy fields surrounding each and every one of us, the energetic pathways of our own human physical bodies, accessible through our inner Spiritual Chakra system, or the energetic ley-lines of the earth.

And why, we may well ask, do our education systems not teach all this?

The answer is obvious! In order to be controlled, we need to be kept in the dark, in ignorance, by those who seek to take our power away from us and manipulate us for their own devious and mercenary ends. We need to be kept dependent on external forces and authorities and not ever allowed access to our own inherent divine nature where we find within ourselves all the answers to all the questions we could ever ask and where we have unlimited potentiality. If this were ever to happen, as indeed it will, if there comes a time, as indeed there will, when we can access our own inherent divine potentiality, then those powers are defunct, obsolete, no longer in control. That's it in a nutshell!

Jesus himself upbraided the teachers of the Law:

"How terrible for you teachers of the Law! You have kept the key that opens the door to the house of knowledge; you yourselves will not go in, and you stop those who are trying to go in!" (Luke 11:52)

But in the time of Jesus and for over 4000 years before that, these ancient Mystery Schools were the teachers of accessing other worlds and energy vibrational levels. But they were not called *'Mystery Schools'* for nothing! They were secretive, mostly passing their teachings down orally, and not written, in order to protect that secrecy, and to ensure that the knowledge did not pass into the wrong hands. And this esoteric, inner knowledge was passed down through symbols. The Gospel of Philip, not included in the canonical gospels confirms this:

'The mysteries of Truth are manifested to us in the form of archetypes or images.' (Gospel of Philip, Plate 132)

And of course, we all know that the ancient Egyptians communicated through symbols in their hieroglyphics, their system of writing and communication where pictures and symbols represented a word or sound. And the Egyptians, as we also know, were deeply ensconced in the ancient Mystery Schools and Mystery Teachings.

Hitler knew well the importance and significance of sacred symbols. He inverted one of the most ancient of sacred symbols, the Antakarana into his Swastika symbol which he used to terrorise Europe. Virgin Atlantic Airlines has the sacred inclusive symbol of the Lemniscate, the figure eight, on the tail of all its aircraft. Most advertisements that flash across our television screens now feature spirals, circles or triangles, all various and diverse aspects of cosmic geometry. And Feng Shui, as we all know, is the art of using the earth's energy lines to build houses and to place objects in a particular position to maximise the natural energy coming from the earth and from surrounding energy fields.

When we talk about *'Enlightened Beings',* we mean those souls amongst us who have already achieved a high degree of Spiritual awareness, raised Spiritual consciousness, Spiritual Enlightenment. These beings exist in the upper echelons of the hierarchy of the Spirit worlds, but they are not detached from us, by any means. We are all connected! We are all connected right across the entire plethora of the different vibrational energy levels throughout the entire spectrum of creation. These already Enlightened beings are no different from us, except that they are further along the path to Enlightenment, and, acknowledging the inter-connectedness of all forms of life, they are devoted to supporting us and helping us attain what they have already attained.

Their influence and inspiration manifest constantly on this material earth plane. Where, for example, do you think all the great scientific discoveries originate? All the great musical masterpieces? All the great art and sculpture works? All the new technological wonders? Yes, they all originate in the soul of each individual genius, and as we will see in a later chapter, the soul is that part of each of us connected to the higher vibrational energy levels. Our soul, depending on its present state of awareness, its present level of raised energy vibration, is either able or not able to receive these transmissions, *"He that hath ears to hear!"* And then these transmissions manifest on this dense energy earth plane. So everything, absolutely everything starts in the Spiritual energy fields, in a higher vibrational frequency, and descends through the mental and the emotional to the physical.

So exactly who are we talking about here? Can we name any of these already Enlightened beings who continue to reach out to us here on Planet Earth, trying to awaken us and raise our Spiritual consciousness?

Well, we have Buddha; Zoroaster of Persia; Lao Tzu of China; the mysterious Magi, fathers of astronomy; Hippocrates, father of modern medicine; Euclid, father of geometry; Pythagoras, whom we read about in the previous chapter; Democritus, father of the atom. Plus, of course, the great philosophers like Pluto, Plato, Thales, Socrates, Aristotle, Heraclitus and many more. All of these were initiates of the ancient Mystery Traditions.

And all down through history, they continue to inspire and influence us here on Planet Earth. Leonardo da Vinci, Isaac Newton, Roger Bacon, William Wordsworth, Walter Raleigh, John Milton, Thomas More, Copernicus, Galileo, William Blake, Botticelli, Victor Hugo, - all have been learned initiates from the ancient Mystery Traditions. All have been at a sufficiently raised soul awareness level to be able to receive and absorb the transmissions from the higher Spiritual energy levels.

And in this time of the Great Awakening following the 2012 realignment of the planets, there is an unprecedented amount of mass higher energies flooding Planet Earth as never before.

So what happened to the Ancient Mystery Schools?

A rapid decline in virtue, morality and spirituality happened! A decline which preceded the destruction of every nation in history. When a nation loses its spirituality, its connection to the whole, its connection to Source, it rapidly declines. The ancient mysteries through time became perverted, those secret societies became infiltrated, sorcery and black witchcraft replacing the divine magic. Hence, today, we have only murmurings of those ancient mysteries remaining.

The adepts and sages of the ancient Mystery Schools fully understood that beneath the world of the five physical senses lies a vastly greater Universal Intelligence. The ancient holders of the knowledge of the mysteries kept everything secret out of respect for that sacred knowledge, and to prevent it from falling into the wrong hands. They understood fully the disastrous effect the mastery of natural forces such as electricity, atomic power and magnetism would have for Planet Earth and indeed the entire Cosmos should such knowledge be usurped and fall into the wrong hands. The ancient Mystery Schools allowed only the most trustworthy and tested students access to this sacred knowledge, and that only after a long period of probationship.

So what was taught in these great Mystery Schools of Greece and India, so strongly connected with the Essenes and the Egyptian Therapeutae?

There were usually three progressive and intense stages of learning, beginning with the Lesser Mysteries, then the Greater Mysteries, and culminating in Mastery.

The Lesser Mysteries concentrated on the whole meaning of life, the nature of life and death, the purpose of man's existence, the inter-connectedness of all forms of life in the great Universal Energy that encompasses all things. The Oneness of all creation and the laws of Karma were all taught through the study of the movement of the stars and planets and the energy pathways of the chakra system of the human body in alignment with the energy leylines of the earth and the energy vibrational frequencies of entire creation. Sciences, mathematics and geometry instilled an understanding of the mechanics of the universe. The whole meaning and working of energy was mastered at this first level, with the student taught how to work within subtle energy fields; how energy attracts like energy and hence the importance of our complete awareness of every thought and word we send out into the universe and into the vast energy network surrounding us on all sides, and how we can control what happens within those subtle energy fields for the good of mankind. And that was the reason for all the secrecy surrounding this sacred knowledge, and ensuring it would not fall into the wrong hands! It could also be used for destruction!

At this first level, the student was also taught to realise his own divine nature and unlimited potentiality. He was taught how to transcend this material physical world, like in near-death experiences and to return to the physical body before the silver cord disconnected, that spiritual cord that connects the soul to the physical body, in just the same way as the umbilical cord connects the babe in the womb to the mother, and is disconnected after birth.

Today, we see this same ability to move in and out of other worlds and vibrational energy levels practised by Shamans and Mystics. I saw myself, in Bali, how young men could induce a deep trance state through dance, and then transcend any physical manifestation of injury or pain inflicted on their bodies, such as knife wounds.

First level students also studied the balance of mind, body and spirit through meditation, toning and chanting, tantric arts or internal energy practices, yogic positions and inter-dimensional contact; biology; botany; healing with herbs; hands-on healing and naturopathy. The supreme teacher was Nature, and close observation of Nature was vital for learning the natural laws and understanding the Divine Feminine. The right and left Eye of Horus were mastered, the right eye representing the masculine and the left eye the feminine.

The Essenes, with whom Jesus was closely connected, were initiated in all of this. Jesus employed these practices when he cast out devils, healed the sick, controlled the forces of nature and even foretold his own Crucifixion.

Certainly a lot for first-level students!

Having mastered the Lesser Mysteries, the student then progressed to the Greater Mysteries.

Here the Divine Masculine was understood. Also the importance of dying to the ego. Of special significance was the learning of spiritual journeys into non-ordinary states of reality, where the student was led through a death-and-rebirth process by being taken, blind-folded, through a series of dark caves or underground passages, where they were forced to confront their deepest fears and where they came into contact through visions, with other higher vibrational energy level entities. Initiates of the Mystery Schools discovered for themselves the secrets of life, death and rebirth. So they saw there was nothing to fear from death.

We have examples of this in Claire Heartsong's book *'Anna, Grandmother of Jesus',* where Jesus himself was led through just such an experience at twelve years of age in Mount Carmel, in what was called the Rite of the Sepulchre, where Jesus experienced the ancient ritual of 'dying' and resurrection. And later, on Mount Sinai, Jesus experienced another initiation. Led blindfolded to the highest crags and left alone without food or water for four days and nights, he was instructed to remain within the circumference of a small circle and to find shelter amongst the stones. He walked in a circular motion while meditating, weaving patterns of sacred geometry, enduring the blazing furnace of the sun during the day and the freezing cold at night. This was, again, an initiation process, where he was exposed to the elements, the four-legged and winged creatures and the demonic and higher celestial energy forces that presented themselves to him in visions and dreams.

Further such initiations were undergone by Jesus in Egypt, this time in the Great Pyramid at Giza, in dark, deep underground passages, again described in detail in Claire Heartsong's book, where Jesus' Spiritual consciousness was further refined, opened to the subtle energies of the mystic, higher realms, and his constitution and character strengthened. The Great Pyramid, described by Heartsong as *"far from serving as a monumental tomb for one of the ancient Egyptian pharaohs, the Great Pyramid was and is, not only an initiation chamber, but also an extraordinarily powerful ascension chamber. It was designed to help initiates awaken to the full remembrance of their true identity. This is the secret of the pyramid."* ('Anna, Grandmother of Jesus' Chapter 32   Page 241)

So these Greater Mysteries taught about the seven dimensional levels of reality, explored the vast cycles of time that govern human evolution and knowledge of worlds within the universe. Physicists today are just rediscovering these multi-dimensional realms that lie beyond our physical senses, but they were known to the mystics of virtually every spiritual tradition in the ancient world.

Finally, the Mastery. This was all about achieving awareness of both the male and female aspects of the Divine, bringing integration and personal balance, which was vital and fundamental to becoming Enlightened. We all have both feminine and masculine aspects to us, having spent numerous life-times as both male and female, balancing these energies within our soul. After becoming integrated and balanced, initiates then committed themselves to the Enlightenment of others. They literally died to their old way, passing beyond surface illusions to the heart of their own divine essence and returned transformed.

"Most assuredly, I say to you, unless you be born again, you cannot see the kingdom of God." (John 3:3)

So in these ancient teachings, the Divine Feminine was extolled, respected and revered. Unfortunately, however, our present-day culture denigrates the Divine Feminine so we have lost the ancient ability to balance the masculine and feminine energies that is required on the earth plane, with the result that our world has thus been out of balance for many centuries. There must be a balance, as in the Gospel of Philip we read: *"Truth is the Mother; knowledge is the Father......"*

And what, if anything at all, do the early writers, philosophers and historians tell us about these Ancient Mysteries?

"While we are encumbered by bodily affections, we can have no intercourse with God..... But when our souls are released (by the Mysteries) and have passed into the region of the pure, invisible and changeless, this God will be our guide and king....." (Plutarch, the Greek historian 46-120 C.E.)

Plato also writes of a *"divine initiation"* through which aspirants *"become spectators of single and blessed visions, residents in a pure light, and are made immaculate and liberated from this surrounding garment which we call the body....."*

As the ancient city of Athens declined, Alexandria was developing on the southern shore of the Mediterranean. In 331 B.C.E. Alexander the Great re-incarnated the spirit of Greece and Athens within his new university in Alexandria. His ancestor, the first Ptolemy, had been a student of Aristotle, and now Grecian, Roman, Persian, Babylonian, Hindu and Jewish teachings and writings were all contained within Alexandria. The works of Homer, Plato, Pythagoras, Aeschylus, Sophocles, Euripides and Aristotle were all available to the great numbers of students who studied and translated the ancient texts. Teachers and students were drawn from across the Eastern worlds, uniting the philosophies of the East and West.

As the larger Mystery Schools gradually declined, they were replaced by smaller '*gnostic*' groups, each of them specialising in keeping alive some special phase of the '*gnosis*', meaning '*ancient knowledge*'.

In Ephesus, Buddhism, Zoroastrianism and the Chaldean system were taught along with the Platonic philosophy, while in Aegea, another gnostic school taught the doctrines of Pythagoras. In Egypt, many of the gnostic schools were affiliated with Judaism, and the Egyptian Mysteries were being perpetuated by the Essenes in their '*lesser*' and '*greater*' mysteries. There was also a Pythagorean branch of the Essenes, known as the '*Koinobi*', as well as the Gymnosophists, while in Egypt, in Alexandria, the Pythagorean group were known as the '*Therapeutae*'.

And indeed, we do not have to go to Egypt and Greece to find these ancient Mystery Schools! We have similar nearer to home! We have the Celtic Druids! All equally ensconced in the ancient Mysteries as the Essenes, with whom Jesus was so strongly connected, and the Egyptian Therapeutae.

Druidic Mystery Schools provided a system of education far in advance of their contemporaries in the rest of the then known continent of Europe, and hence Gallic students sought philosophical learning and training at the Druid Schools in Britain. These too were cloaked in secrecy, like the ancient Mystery Schools of Greece and Egypt, the knowledge being handed down orally to specially prepared and tested candidates, in order to protect it from falling into the wrong hands.

Scholars differ in where these Druidic Mysteries originated. Some speculate that the Druidic priests obtained their wisdom from Phoenician and Tyrian sea navigators visiting the Isles of Britain thousands of years before the time of Jesus, searching for tin. It is widely reported that the young Jesus made frequent trips with his uncle, Joseph of Arimathea, himself a tin merchant, his large fleet of ships plying back and forth across the Mediterranean as far as southern Britain, bringing back tin for use in weaponry for the vast expanding Roman armies. It was during such voyages that Jesus spent time being initiated into the Druidic Mysteries. Other scholars maintain that Druidic Mysteries were of Oriental origin, possibly Buddhistic.

Before a candidate was admitted and instructed in the secret doctrines of the Druids, he was sworn to secrecy, the teachings and knowledge being imparted only in deep forests and dark caves. Here, far from other men, the student was instructed in the creation of the universe, the laws of nature, the secrets of medicine, the mysteries of the celestial bodies, and magic and sorcery.

Like nearly all schools of the Ancient Mysteries, the teachings of the Druids were divided into distinct phases. The most simple of these teachings, a moral code, was taught to all the people, while the deeper, esoteric, inner doctrines were reserved for only initiated priests. A candidate had to be from a reputable family and of high moral character, and no important secret teachings were entrusted to him until he had passed various tests of temptation and strength of character. The Druids taught the immortality of the soul, transmigration of the soul between worlds and reincarnation, as well as the Laws of Karma, cause and effect. They had a deep understanding of Nature and her laws. They studied geography, physical science, natural theology and astrology. They had a fundamental knowledge of medicine, especially the use of herbs and plants. They cured by magnetism and charging amulets and jewellery with healing energies.

The first known text that describes the Druids is Julius Caesar's *'Commentarii de Bello Gallico'* Book vi, written in the 50s or 40s B.C.E. A military general who was intent on conquering Gaul and Britain, Caesar described the Druids as being concerned with *"divine worship, the due performance of sacrifices, private or public, and the interpretation of ritual questions."*

Caesar claimed that the Druids played an important part in Gaulish society and that they performed the function of judges. They viewed Britain as the centre of Druidic learning, and students had to learn all the Druidic lore by heart. Their main teaching, according to Caesar, was that *"souls do not perish, but after death pass from one to another"*. They were also concerned with *"the stars and their movements, the size of the cosmos and the earth, the world of nature, and the powers of deities."*

"It is they who decide in almost all disputes, public and private; and if any crime has been committed, or murder done, or there is any dispute about succession or boundaries, they also decide it, determining rewards and penalties: if any person or people does not abide by their decision, they ban such from sacrifice, which is their heaviest penalty." (Caesar: 'Gallic Wars')

"A great number of young men gather about them for the sake of instruction and hold them in great honour.......Report says that in the schools of the Druids they learn by heart a great number of verses, and.........they do not think it proper to commit these utterances to writing, although in almost all other matters, and in their public and private accounts, they make use of Greek letters." (Caesar: 'Gallic Wars')

Other classical writers also commented on the Druids and their practices. Cicero, for example, a contemporary of Caesar's, commented on how the Druids knew much about the natural world and performed divination.

Diodorus Siculus, writing about 36 B.C.E. viewed the Druids as philosophers and theologians, with many poets and songsters in Celtic society, called *'bards'*.

Tacitus, the Roman writer, a senator and historian, described how in a battle against the Romans when the Romans attacked Anglesey, the Druids, with hands uplifted towards the sky, poured down such torrents of curses and *"terrible imprecations"* on the heads of the invaders. He states that these *"terrified our soldiers who had never seen such a thing before..."*

The Druids included philosophers, theologians, priests, judges, guarantors of political institutions, educators of the young and magicians. And it is clear from most sources that the Druids were teachers, teaching at both an esoteric and exoteric level. Their teachings were based on the five elements: earth, sea, sky, sun and moon. They were also seers and wonderworkers, of unusual skills.

"Some say that the study of philosophy was of barbarian origin. For

the Persians had their Magi, the Babylonians or the Assyrians the Chaldeans, the Indians their Gymnosophists, while the Kelts and the Galatae had seers called Druids....." (Diogenes Laertius: 'Lives of the Philosophers' circa 250 C.E.)

A Druid usually had one or more students living in his household, in just the same as a Jewish Rabbi would have had a Talmudic School. It is recorded that in Ulster, Cathbad, the chief Druid at the court of King Conor MacNeasa had over one hundred students at any one time. The relationship between the king and Druid was of extreme importance. The Druid's favourite tree was the Rowan tree, for it was under the Rowan tree that he would sleep, in order to gain prophetic visions from his dreams.

Students in the Druidic schools were taught philosophy, law, magic, healing skills, divination, the sciences, chemistry, alchemy, astronomy, astrology, mathematics and numerology. The stone circles that they built required exact and sophisticated measuring, calculating and engineering skills and depended upon a deep knowledge of the movement of the planets. It was their knowledge and skill in astronomy that enabled them to build Newgrange and Stonehenge, the same skills that enabled the pyramids in Egypt to be built.

And 2000 years ago, it was in the gnostic schools, all of which were remnants of the Ancient Mystery Schools, that Jesus received his knowledge and was initiated into the ancient rites. He was definitely initiated into the secrets of the Egyptian Mysteries through the Pythagorean branch of the Essenes, evidenced by the fact that most of the teachings attributed to Jesus are in the Pythagorean spirit.

So the Essene Brotherhood did indeed have its roots firmly grounded in the ancient Mystery Schools. They were a Jewish sect representing an esoteric aspect of Judaism or Jewish mysticism.

Yes, Jesus' teachings were built around the ancient mysteries and initiations! Even his method of teaching in parables! The use of parable, story and myth was a powerful teaching device employed by the Egyptian Schools, whose initiates even encoded their hieroglyphic writings on three different levels, so they could be understood by all, delivering different meanings depending on the reader's level of esoteric training. And Jesus was taught in those Egyptian schools!

So we can clearly see that a lot has been left out of Western Christianity about Jesus' participation in the mystery traditions. Jesus was trained in the Mysteries. His life and miracles, which were performed in accordance with natural law, show that he had discovered the invisible secrets behind the world of form and matter.

But now let us return to Pythagoras and the Music of the Spheres, Pythagoras being a product of these Ancient Mystery Schools and teachings, and put all this into the context of the musical compositions of Pat McCourt, or indeed any composer, poet or artist.

Chapter 3:

Body and Soul

We *have* a body. But we *are* a soul.

We are first and foremost spiritual beings, spiritual beings having a physical experience for the duration of this life-time. We have experienced many previous life-times and we will no doubt experience many more. Eternity is not something which just starts after we pass over or transition back to Spirit. This is eternity, the here and now, and this present life-time is just one of our many walk-abouts across the vastness of infinity, across the fathomless expanse of eternity. We are spiritual, galactic travellers, journeying throughout the entire cosmos, traversing the infinity of creation, transcending time and space.

Our soul, our divine spirit, is immortal. It will never die or cease to be. Our body, on the other hand, is merely the casing, the wrapping, the outward visible layer through which we present ourselves to the world, and through which most people recognise us and see us to be. Just as we discard an old, worn-out coat when we have no further need for it or when it has outlived its present usefulness, so too, the physical body in which we have our soul encased for the duration of this life-time, we will also discard. It has served its present purpose. We no longer need it. We are in the process of transitioning back to Spirit, from whence we have all come, and we have no further need of a physical body. Our soul disconnects from our physical body at the point of transition, with our last breath, and expands outwards along a silver cord. When that silver cord snaps or disconnects, that silver cord that connects our body to our soul, then that is the point of no return for us back into our physical body. We are on our way home! Again!

Our physical body is connected to this physical world, this earthly plane, through our five physical senses. These are the mechanisms through which we are able to experience this world. We see, we hear, we touch, we taste, we smell. We cease to do any of these when we transition back to Spirit, because these are merely physical attributes, appertaining to and belonging to our physical body only.

Our physical body is surrounded on all sides by an energy field called our aura. Every form of life has its own aura attached to it. Plants, trees, flowers, animals, people, all are surrounded by a three-dimensional electro-magnetic energy field, in an oval shape like an egg. Our aura is constantly changing, depending on the thoughts we are sending out, the emotions we are feeling at any one time, the physical condition of our body, and is constantly interacting with the auric fields of others around us. No two of our auras are the same, and that is why when a Reiki or other holistic treatment is given, no two of us experience the same. The divine energy with which the practitioner is connecting, is of course the same for each of us, but when that divine energy connects with all our individual and unique auras, then it obviously produces a different effect for each one of us.

Every thought, every emotion, every feeling, all go outwards into our aura. Notice how, when you meet someone, you connect with them in either a positive way or in a negative way. Some people give you an instant lift, boosting your energy, while others drag you down, leaving you depleted and wondering what just happened! An energy vampire! That's what just happened! A hungry vampire looking for a feed, a fix! And you just happened to come along! Divine timing or what!

And just as our aura interconnects with the auras of others, so too, the auras of plants, flowers, trees and in fact everything in nature, interconnect with each other. And yes, they interconnect with us as well! Constantly! That's why spending time in nature is so therapeutic for us.

And what we send out through our aura attracts the same back to us. That's the irrefutable, the indisputable, the inviolable law of the universe,- like attracts like! A clear, clean high vibration aura attracts back to it other clear, clean high vibration auras. Conversely, a dark, weak, lower vibration aura magnetises to it other dark, weak, lower vibration auras. There is an anomaly here however! Whilst dark auras attract only dark auras, bright clean auras on the other hand, whilst magnetising other clean bright auras to them, also fall prey to dark auras. And why? Because dark auras are looking for their energy fix! Energy vampires! And then along you come, your aura shining brightly! Of course they have you spotted! Like moths to a flame, like bees to the honey pot, they have registered you on their radar!

Just as our five physical senses connect us to the physical world around us, so too, we have what is called our chakra system which connects us to all things spiritual.

Just as the earth itself has energy lines, called ley lines running through it, so too we have our chakras, the energy centres of our etheric body, and they connect us to the universe, to the greater energy field of All That Is. They have been described by Jung as '**the gateways of consciousness**'.

We have seven chakras in all, aligned vertically, from the base of our spine to the crown of our head, running vertically along our spine, spinning and rotating like a Catherine wheel, each chakra a different colour and each chakra related to a particular aspect of ourselves. This alignment of our seven chakra system along our spine reflects our upward spiritual development, as we raise our consciousness from our base need for survival, from our base chakra, to our connection to Spirit, through our crown chakra.

Our chakras, just like our aura, send out energy waves that return to us, attracting people of similar minds into our aura. For example, if we suffer from addiction problems, alcohol, gambling, drugs, our sacral chakra, our second chakra from the bottom, sends out the messages and we attract other alcoholics and drug users into our lives. On the other hand, if we are highly spiritually aware, our crown chakra, our connection to the divine, to Spirit, emits the signals, and we magnetise people to us who are on a similar spiritual path to our own.

All of our seven chakras are connected, all attached to each other through an energy wave mechanism or system, in the form of the figure eight, known as the Infinity Sign or the Lemniscate. And as we saw earlier, it is this figure eight or Leminiscate that is on the tail of every Virgin Atlantic airplane. Richard Branson certainly understands its meaning and its power!

Music of the Spheres

When we listen to the musical compositions of McCourt as he plays, what is happening is that various Leminiscate energy waves move through each of our chakras in turn, producing an overall resonant response within our body. As each human body is a microcosm of the macrocosm of the Great Universal Energy, the Great Universal God Consciousness, All That Is, then this resonant response flows not only through our own human body via our chakra system, but also connects to the universe beyond our physicality. Hence, we experience a rise in consciousness and a connection to All That Is, a feeling of being at One with the universe and all creation. But it is what McCourt himself sends out through his chakra system and his aura, in those waves of energy emanating from him, that initiates the whole process. Remember! Like attracts like! That irrefutable law of the universe! And only if we are ready and able to raise our spiritual consciousness to a higher level, then and only then can any of this actually happen.

This explains why each piece of music appeals to some of us, but not to all of us. It's all got to do with making that connection, starting with the musician, through the physical human chakra system, to our own soul and what lies beyond.

What the musician sends out either resonates with us or it does not. If it does, then it is literally a case of **all systems go**! If it does not resonate with us, then we simply move on to another piece of music that does.

All the sages, the great writers, the poets, the artists, the musicians, all sought and found peace and quiet in certain places in Nature, all in order to feed the creativity that lay within. William Percy French sought and found this elusive peace and tranquillity in Wales, after the untimely death of his first wife Ettie in childbirth, at only eighteen years of age and after only a year and a day of marriage, their baby daughter following her just a few weeks later. In Wales, where he spent a year painting, French connected with his own soul and his own spirituality through his paintings. William Butler Yeats found it in County Sligo, his '*place of the heart*'. And so too, all the great Romantic poets, for example, William Wordsworth, who found it in the Lake District, one of the most beautiful parts of England. But times are different now! Industrialization, urbanization, pollution, desecration, extractions, mining, deforestation, all have taken their toll on our beautiful planet and we now need to travel further afield to find that peace and tranquillity for which we all thirst.

McCourt too finds nourishment and solace in quiet, remote and unspoilt places on the earth, far from the maddening crowd and far from suffocating and ear-shattering commercialism and industrialization. This is what feeds his soul, so this is what he is sending out as he plays, in the form of energy waves, and we pick that up, but only if our aura and chakra system are on a similar wave length.

To watch and listen to McCourt play, therefore, is to become part of the Music of the Spheres, that musical harmony, according to the ancients,- Pythagoras, Plato and Aristotle, that is emitted as the sun, the moon and the planets all rotate in orbit, sending out a sound, a vibration, and when we connect to that Universal Harmony, that musical vibration, for that is what each musical note is, a vibration, an energy vibration, it is then that we experience that peace, that feeling of complete Oneness for which we yearn, simply because it is the energy vibration from whence we have come, to which we yearn to return, and to where we will all eventually return.

And as we watch and listen to McCourt play, we are making that divine connection.

We will see in a later chapter the further effects that music has on our physical body and, therefore, on our aura and on our chakra system, and how that in turn affects all those around us. But first, we need to consider ***what we are*** and how our understanding of what we are is indeed crucial to understanding the whole meaning of life and why we are here. It cannot be, surely that we are just meant to be born and then to die? There must be more to it all than that!

And there *is* more to it! ***A lot more!***

Chapter 4:

What we are

Energy! That is what we all **are**. And energy is **all** that we are!

Everything in the entirety of creation is made up of energy in some form or other. The only difference between any of us and all of the various forms of energy is the frequency on which each one vibrates.

And energy never dies. It cannot be killed off. It cannot be terminated. So we cannot end. But energy can be changed. It can be transmuted. In fact it is constantly changing and transmuting. And that is exactly what we do. We transmute to a higher, lighter form of energy. We metamorphose into a higher energy vibration. Like the caterpillar and the butterfly, once the caterpillar metamorphoses into a butterfly, it is no longer a caterpillar, it can no longer be a caterpillar, it can never again return to being a caterpillar.

As energy, we never end. There is no death. There is only a transition to a higher form of energy. All the great sages, poets and artists knew this. William Percy French knew it, as we can clearly see from his poems written on the death of his first wife Ettie, *'Not Lost But Gone Before'* and *'Only Goodnight.'* The metaphysical poets of the Medieval ages knew it, as seen in John Donne's poem *'Death Thou Shalt Die'*.

At some stage in our life, there comes a time when we each get a wake-up call, something that happens to us that causes us to pause and consider the whole meaning of our existence and what lies beyond our own physicality. The wake-up call for William Percy French came with the death of Ettie, and marked a clear watershed in his life, changing him from a happy-go-lucky character to a much more serious person. Even his hair turned from brown to white over a period of just one year. And his poem, with the very explicit title *'Here and Hereafter'* was written as the result of that wake-up call.

There are limitless numbers of energy vibrational frequencies all around us. Just like the radio or television, when we are listening to one channel, the other channels have not gone away anywhere. They are still there, all around us, we are just not tuned into them.

The Music of the Spheres can only be understood in terms of energy, in terms of the multitude of energy vibrational frequencies that constantly surround us. As we have already seen, Pythagoras taught that all the planets as they rotate throughout the entirety of creation, all vibrate on a particular frequency, a particular energy vibrational frequency. Every word we speak, every sound we make, every thought we have, as well as every action we perform, all go out into the ether as energy waves, joining the Great Universal Energy Stream. And there are no straight lines in the Great Universal Energy Stream. All energy is recycled. It never dies or ends. Music, like everything else in the entirety of creation, is a vibrational energy on a certain frequency, so the vibrational energy that William Percy French sent out through his melodies is still out there. When McCourt plays William Percy French, it is this frequency into which he is tapping.

Remember, we attract to us what we send out! That's the irrefutable law of the universe!

Then when McCourt himself composes, he is sending out a new vibration, and the harmonious sounds he emits through the piano merge with this Greater Universal Energy Field embellishing and enhancing, and at the same time balancing with the more raucous, nerve-shattering sounds that are also sent out there, such as cries of agony and distress, shouts of rage and anger, words of bitterness and hatred. It is all a matter of balance. Everything is perfectly balanced in our world, in our universe and throughout all of creation. Those harsh, offensive sounds that are sent out there by us on their own vibrational frequency are negative and cumbersome, trundling along in the Great Universal Energy Stream. Then the harmonious sounds sent out on their vibrational frequency, being positive and lighter, also join the Universal Energy Stream. But because they are travelling more quickly, due to their higher, lighter vibration, they will catch up with the heavier more cumbersome vibrations and transmute them all into lighter, higher vibrational energy. Simple, really!

Now before you ask, why do the heavier vibrational energy frequencies not transmute the lighter energy vibrational frequencies, let me explain! When you go into a dark room, how do you get rid of the dark? By bundling it all up into a bag and taking it away? Hardly! You don't get rid of it at all, in fact. You turn on the light, and that changes, or transmutes, the darkness into light. But it does not kill or end the darkness. It just transmutes it into light, and when you turn the light off again, the darkness is still there. It has not gone anywhere!

That is how all energy works! We are all energy. Music, like everything else in the entirety of creation is energy, vibrating on a particular frequency, going out there into the ether, merging with the Great Universal Energy Stream, the Great Universal God Energy, the Great Universal God Consciousness, and bringing harmony and balance to counteract the harsh, raucous, era-splitting, nerve-shattering sounds that are sent out there as well.

Chapter 5:

The One Great Universal Consciousness

The sum of all the energy frequencies in the entirety of creation, that ever have been, that are and ever will be is what we call the Great Universal Energy, the Great Universal Consciousness. Or in one word, God. There is only One Universal Breath, One Universal Heart-beat, One Universal Pulse. And we are all connected as One within that Great One Universal Consciousness, that One Great Universal God Energy, outside of which nothing and no-one can have any existence.

Think of the wave in the ocean. The wave has no existence outside of the ocean. The wave is only there because the ocean has thrown it up, the ocean has given life to it. The wave builds up in intensity and volume and then crashes. It is no longer a wave, but it is still in the ocean. There is no other place it can be. It still *IS* the ocean. It has now just changed energy form within that same ocean.

So too with us. We have no place or existence outside of the Great Universal God Energy.

Again, dip your hand in the ocean and take a small droplet of water on your finger. That tiny droplet of water is not the ocean in the ocean's entirety, but it still contains all the elements of the ocean within it. It has the watery texture, it has the salty taste.

So too with us. Each one of contains within our own being, all the elements of the Great Universal God Energy, but no one of us on our own is God in God's entirety.

Picture a fog. Within that fog, shapes emerge and retreat, continuously changing form, changing shape, but always remaining within the fog. There is no place else for them to go! There is no place else for them to have any existence. For it is the fog that has thrown them up, the fog itself is the only reason for their very existence.

So too with us. We have no other place to go, no other place to be outside of the Great Universal God Energy.

And within that Great Universal God Energy, there is a consciousness in all living things, each a microcosm of the macrocosm that is entire creation, that Great Universal Consciousness.

The whole of creation is held together in large part through the most sophisticated system of sound. A cacophany of sound, a great cosmic orchestral extravaganza, a harmonious blending of vibrational energy frequencies being constantly emitted out into the ether by us and other forms of life, merging with the Great Universal God Energy Field. Everything has a sound, the earth itself, stars, even empty space. And even silence! **'The sound of silence'.**

All material objects, including ourselves, are vibrations of frequencies and sound tones. The theory of the Big Bang, believed by many is that theory that the Big Bang was the beginning, or one of the beginnings, of these frequencies. Light, sound, and material objects all vibrate to various frequencies, just like musical notes do.

So, really, everything is music! Music is everything! A great symphony! Music wafts on the breeze, it flows in rivers and streams, it is in the bird songs, it is heard in the sighing of the winds, the crashing of the waves on the shore, the plopping of the raindrops, even in the dripping of your tap. Some of the notes, however, are just too high or too low for the human ear to hear!

The ancient philosopher Aristotle explains why none of us can hear the musical sounds even though they are of a great magnitude:

'The sound is in our ears from the very moment of birth and is thus indistinguishable from its contrary silence, since sound and silence are discriminated by mutual contrast'.

An analogy can be drawn with the blacksmith, who spends all of his time surrounded by the din of his anvil, until finally he grows oblivious to it.

Likewise, if we surround ourselves, as we do, with constant noise, then of course we cannot hear the hum of the universe!

The sonar calls of the whales and dolphins, the bird song, the lapping of the waters, the crashing of the waves on the shore, the whispers of the breeze, the messages carried on the winds, the rustle of the trees, the scrunch of the autumn leaves, the barking of a dog, the laughter of a child, every sound you can think of and which we hear every day, all go out into the ether on vibrational energy waves, joining the Great Universal God Consciousness, the Great Universal God Energy Stream.

And there are no straight lines in the Great Universal God Energy Field! Just as there are no straight lines in Nature. Everything is cyclical, coming round time and time again, into and throughout infinity.

And everything, every single consciousness within that Great Universal Consciousness is in rhythm. Everything in life has a rhythm, a beat, as do the planets, as do our bodies. That rhythm has an ebb and flow, which can be affected by our states.

'The rhythm of life is a powerful beat! Feel the tingle in your fingers, feel the tingle in your feet!'

And it is all the One rhythm! There is One Universal Rhythm. The One Cosmic Orchestra. The One Universal Harmony. In essence, the universe can be considered as 'One Song'. And it is music that connects us to this Great Universal God Energy, where everything is in rhythm. Music opens for us the vibrational corridor into higher, expanded states of consciousness.

Have you ever noticed, as you walk alongside someone, what automatically happens, without you even thinking about it? How you both automatically fall into synch with other?

Or if you place your hand on someone's heart, and they place their hand on your heart, how you both begin to breathe in synch? How your two heart-beats begin to beat as one?

All the words we speak, all the poetry ever written, all beats to a ryhthm. That's what full stops and commas, that which we call punctuation, does. Punctuation creates a rhythm. In poetry, which is really words without music, all poets fall into a rhythm pattern. Shakespeare's main claim to fame is that every single line of his entire verse and poetry, in all his plays, was written in iambic pentameter, that particular rhythm of five strong beats to every line. Other poets use alternative rhythm meters, such as for example iambic trimeter, three strong beats to every line, or iambic tetrameter, which is four strong beats to every line, the rhythm always reflecting the mood or the emotions of the poet.

Rhythm is a beat. A beat is music. Music is Spirit. Spirit is eternal. Spirit is everything there is. Whether it is the rhythm of the waves crashing on the shore, the drone of your car engine, the chugging of a train along the tracks, the clanging of a blacksmith's hammer, or whatever, everything is part of the Great Cosmic Dance, the Great Cosmic Rhythm.

The Harmony of the Spheres! It was Pythagoras who identified three sorts of music, three sorts of harmony, in his philosophy known as '**Musica Universalis**'. First, he identified 'Musica Instrumentalis', the ordinary music made by any musical instrument. Secondly, 'Musica Humana', the continuous but unheard music made by each human organism, especially the harmonious or even the unharmonious resonance between the soul and the body, and thirdly, 'Musica Mundana', the music made by the cosmos itself, as the planets continue to revolve on their orbital path.

When McCourt plays, the harmonious melody he sends out into the ether, harmonious because, as we will see in the next chapter, it is coming directly from his own Higher Self, that part of him that is his own God Essence in its most pure, highest form, that highest vibrational frequency into which he tunes when he plays, then those sounds he emits through the piano, blend in and merge with this great cosmic orchestral extravaganza. Like everything else we send out, it all returns to us in an even more enhanced harmonious way, uplifting us, raising our own vibration, giving us that feel-good factor, sending us on our way about our daily tasks with a lightness in our step, love in our heart and a deep knowing that we are tapped into something greater than ourselves, something way beyond our physical sensory mechanism, beyond that which we can experience through our limited five physical senses.

And as McCourt connects with this Great Universal God Energy, this Great Universal Rhythm, in the Symphony Of All Life, we who are listening, we too are connecting, through him, to this Great Universal Rhythm. That is why our feet begin to tap, our body starts to sway, as we fall into synch with that Great One Universal Rhythm.

And to be able to play music, especially straight from the heart, as does McCourt, then that is essentially an act of releasing positive, high vibrational frequency energy out into the world, high vibrational frequency energy which will return to us time and time again, bringing us only joy and pleasure. What better good could any of us do for our Planet Earth? And indeed, what could ever be any more spiritual?

Chapter 6:

The Soul and the Higher Self

Your Soul is the overall you, you in your entirety, you in your totality. It is what you are. Everything you are, everything you ever have been and everything you ever will be is incorporated into your Soul.

What is the difference between your Soul and your Higher Self?

Your Soul is the **sole** reason for you being on this earth plane. Each time you come into a new incarnation on this physical earth plane, you do not need to take all of your Soul with you. You only need to take the small proportion required for this life-time, to get you through this life-time only and to learn the lessons you yourself have chosen to learn during this life-time in order to advance your immortal Soul. When you incarnate on this physical earth plane, you are descending to a lower vibrational energy level, the level of matter and physicality.

The greater proportion of your Soul remains in the higher vibrational energy levels within the whole Great Universal Energy which we call God. That is your Higher Self, your own God Essence in its highest, most pure form.

As the highest, purest form of your God Essence, your Higher Self knows the answer to every question you could ever possibly ask. It is your own Higher Self which guides, enlightens and inspires you through life. We saw in an earlier chapter that God is not a physical being, or indeed a being of any sort. God is energy, the Great Universal God Energy, outside of which nothing and no-one can have any sort of existence.

And when we pray, what are we doing? Praying to an external God who will grant some requests and refuse others? But as we have seen there is no external God to whom we can pray! So what happens then when we pray?

When we pray, we are connecting with our own Higher Self, our own God Essence in its purest highest form, and it is our own God Essence, our own Higher Self sending us the answers. Our own Higher Self within the Great Universal God Energy, our own Higher Self that inspires, directs and guides us.

When McCourt is playing, he is connecting with his own Higher Self, that part of him that is his own God Essence in its purest, highest form. The channel from his own Higher Self is opened and the inspiration flows through naturally. But he cannot ever compose anything until that same channel is opened.

And why not? Why can he not just sit down any time and compose a piece of music? Surely it must be that simple?

The answer lies in the fact that the creative process within him, as within each of us, is a receptive process and not an active process. It cannot be produced on demand or to order. It just begins to flow through of its own accord. Flowing from the higher vibrational energy frequency, where McCourt's soul unites with that pure God Essence, where he makes that resonant connection, where he joins with the Music of the Spheres, the One Great Universal Breath, that One Great Universal Pulse, that One Great Universal Heart-beat. For there is only One!

Yes, music and spirituality reinforce each other, each being a bridge to the other. Spirituality is connecting with that which lies beyond our five physical senses, our limited physical sensory mechanism. Music is the path that connects us to our own Higher Self, that part of us that is our God essence in its highest, most pure form. And the path that connects us to the other higher realms throughout the entirety of creation.

Chapter 7:

Beyond our five physical senses

There is much more in creation than what we can sense through the limited sensory mechanism of our five physical senses.

We are only one universe amongst many. We live in a world of matter, on a lower, more dense vibration than the vast multitude of other worlds and energy frequency levels surrounding us, many of which are millions of light years ahead of us.

2012 marked a great energy shift in our planetary system. For the first time in 26,000 years, and for only the second time in 260,000 years, the planets in our entire galaxy aligned in a specific format that raised the energy vibration of our Planet Earth to a much higher level. It is no coincidence, for there is no such thing, that since 2012, more and more of the higher energy vibrational frequencies are making themselves known to us here on Planet Earth. The veil between worlds is thinning rapidly, as more and more of us are beginning to be able to make that connection with other vibrational frequencies, with what we call the Spirit worlds.

Yes, we are a microcosm of the macrocosm of entire creation. And as such, we are surrounded by all the other microcosms. We cannot see or hear them, but they are there. We are talking here about the spirits of Nature, of course. Call them the Fairy Folk, the Little Folk, the Elementals, whatever, but they are there! Our ancestors were much more in tune with them than we are now, surrounded as we are by constant noise in this modern world.

William Percy French and William Butler Yeats, two of Ireland's literary greats, were certainly well tuned into the Fairy worlds that surround us on all sides, as we shall see in later chapters. As were indeed all the literary greats throughout the centuries. These were all conscious of other energies and presences all around, and they were able to tap into those energies.

Gerard Manley Hopkins, in '*God's Grandeur*' wrote:

'Look at the Stars! Look, look up at the skies! O look at all the fire-folk sitting in the air! The bright boroughs, the circle-citadels there! Down in dim woods the diamond delves! The elves' eyes!'

The metaphysical poet of the middle ages, John Donne, too, was aware of all the subtle worlds in our coherent, connected, universe:

'I am a little world made cunningly of elements.'

Yes! There is a whole world of elementals out there, beyond the normal vision of most human eyes, but visible to those who have opened their hearts and souls to nature. Many of us cannot see even the physical and the obvious around us, let alone the reality beyond our five physical senses! The world of nature's elementals, the whole intricate fabric of the fairy world, the constant activity going on amongst nature's little minders, the guardians, the nurturers, the life forces that sustain the Greatest Show on Earth. The elemental kingdom influences absolutely everything we see around us, under our feet, above our heads, the very air we breathe. They have been healing our world for thousands of years, all unsung heroes, and all the time having their territory encroached upon, with less and less room for them to exist.

Religions down through history have tended to repress people's awareness of the spirits around us in nature. Witches were burned at the stake or drowned because of their knowledge. Likewise, pagans were repressed as being evil doers, whereas, in fact, they actually acknowledged and honoured the spirits in all forms of life. But life is changing, and we all, instinctively, deep down, know that we all have a deep basic connection with the spirits of nature. The old Druidic customs are once again becoming acknowledged, as we rediscover that working with spirits is part of our spiritual path, and that the world needs us to work with these spirits.

It is our lower based human ego that tells us such entities as devas, fairies, fairy queens, elementals, unicorns, dragons, orbs, pixies, gnomes etc., do not exist. They have all been recorded, and written about and spoken about in folklore and history, but our modern day minds have shut them out, we have turned our backs on anything we cannot experience with our physical senses. It was not always that way, however. Our grandparents and great grandparents knew about the fairy creatures who inhabited our landscape, the devic life that surrounded them and permeated their daily life. For many of us today, the best we can come up with is the tooth fairy! We are oblivious to the ordered, structured subtle energies that form the orchestra for the Great Cosmic Dance of Nature. All the four elements, water, fire, earth and air, have elementals and fairies looking after them, all working to a highly structured plan. The earth and air elementals look like Tinkerbell, with transparent wings and bodies which change colour depending on what they are doing and where they are. The water spirits, who work and heal using the power of water, are called undines, water spirits and sylphs. The fairies who work with fire energy are the salamanders, very powerful and very magical! Watch a young child gazing into a fire, totally mesmerized, totally bewitched. What he is seeing, you may ask. Look for yourself and see! See the dancing, swirling colours, the shapes that form before your very eyes. And then tell me it is not indeed magic! The same with water. Why do so many people sit staring out over the sea? You tell me!

These forms of life all do exist, in a higher vibration than humans, as a different form of energy, and, like all forms of life, a manifestation of the Divine. They will choose when and where they let us see them. It is never our choice. We are the lower vibration, they the higher. When we have raised our consciousness sufficiently to make an encounter possible, then it will happen. When we have reached a certain level of spiritual maturity, they will reveal themselves to us. But know for certain, they are there! We have ample evidence of, for example, orbs in photography, so why do we still doubt? Many more of us are tapping into the angelic kingdom, but still we seem unwilling to accept the reality of the fairy kingdom.

The same energy that keeps us alive, the same energy that keeps animals alive, also keeps all of nature alive! Everything vibrates with universal energy, which shows in our aura. All living life forms in nature have an aura. The human eye can be trained to see it. Using your peripheral vision, look just beyond the edge of a tree or plant. Soften your gaze, and you will see a grey coloured mist, a haze surrounding the tree. That is the aura. With practice, you will also begin to see colours.

Your garden, and all green areas, are mystical, magical places. To connect with the spirit of any tree or plant, give it a personality. If it were a person, what would it be like? The trees in my garden, like all trees and plants everywhere all have a different, unique personality, and in seeing that, I am connecting with the spirit of each tree, with the elementals that nurture and care for each branch, each leaf, and with the deva, the overall spiritual guardian of each tree. I have two variegated poplar trees, one each side of my garden, that blossom in beautiful peach and white leaves each year. Those two trees just know they are so pretty; they are just so full of themselves! They try to outdo each other in getting attention, as if telling all the other trees *'Look at me!' Look how pretty I am!'* My rose trees, on the other hand, also know they are beautiful, but they don't flaunt their beauty or flounce about in front of the others. They are very elegant and they keep themselves to themselves, confident in letting their beauty speak for itself. My cherry trees, the first to blossom each Spring, spread themselves out into everybody else's territory, as if to say *'I'm only going to blossom for a short while, so I want to be noticed now!'* Then at the bottom of the garden I have a beautiful Canadian pineapple tree that just flops about all over the place. Yes, each has a different personality and I can sense that as I bring the hose down to water them at the end of a long, hot, summer's day. I feel each calling to me *'Over here! ....Ah! ....That's good!'* Being with them, is relaxing and peaceful, their energy can definitely be felt.

Every blade of grass, every leaf, has an elemental looking after it; every flower has an elemental over-lighting it and bringing it to perfection. Each elemental holds the blue-print, the energy pattern of the perfect flower. Each elemental or fairy exists to nurture, encourage and draw its charge towards perfection. In the novel, *'The Colour Purple',* in answer to Celie's question *'How that (colour purple) get there?'* the colours in the flowers, in all of nature, are brought to them by the nature spirits, the fairies, the elementals, working through the central stem of the plants, or trunk of the tree, pouring in their own essence, expressing their own consciousness, their own character, through the manifestation of the flower, leaf or tree. Divine light is pulsating everywhere, channelled by the elemental beings, flooding our world with Divine light and love, performing the Greatest Show on Earth. The magic that is constantly going on all around us! The wonder, the interconnection, the intertwining of the movements in the choreography of the Great Cosmic Dance! Spirits and fairies, like us, are learning from their experiences, as they too seek to raise their spiritual consciousness to 'graduate' into higher dimensions. And it is all rigidly controlled, ordered and structured. Each rose petal, for example, has an elemental; the rose tree has a deva controlling the elementals; and all the rose devas have a Rose Angel in charge of them.

There is a loving, Divine Plan at work holding all this together, and not only in nature, but in our physical bodies as well. Each of us has a deva overlooking our entire body, while each and every organ, vein, bone, tissue, part, has an elemental or elementals looking after it. What a plan! What a tapestry! What a magical, swirling, twirling, dance of life! No human brain could think that all out!

Music of the Spheres

Only Divine Plan could have come up with that one! The interconnectedness of us all, the dependency of us all on each other, as we each and all strive to raise our vibration to find our way back to Source. The intricate, intriguing, criss-crossing, mindboggling web of life! And we're all in it! We cannot advance spiritually, or get spiritual 'promotion' on our own. We must take all others with us. We are all climbing the mountain, walking the road, but we are all at different stages of that process. No one of us is any greater, or lesser than any other. We are all going to end up in the same place, eventually, back home with Source. But we all need each other to advance our own spiritual awareness, and the spiritual awareness of all forms of life and of entire humanity.

The tiny entities that work ceaselessly amongst our trees, plants, flowers and grass are as real as we are. When I ask the elementals of the grass, to *'go take a hike, please!'* for a short time while I walk on their territory, I can feel a change in the atmosphere, in the energy. As they withdraw temporarily, a sort of hush, an emptiness, falls over everything. They return, of course, when I finish my job, and everything seems to be filled with life again. Which of course it is!

During nights of a full moon, the activity in your garden is intensified. It is then that the party really gets under way! No one could question the magical effect of the Moon! You can feel its magic and power if you just stand for a while and gaze at it, allowing its feminine energy to soak into you. A full moon is a great time to re-charge and cleanse your crystals. They will certainly thank you for it! A full moon is also a great time to send your prayers and wishes out into the universe, as they will be enhanced and fortified by the full moon's vibration and energy. You must, at some stage of your life, have experienced the magic of moonlit nights. The sparkling, dazzling, dancing of the water's surface as it responds to the energy from the moon! The pull of the moon is strong, on the tide, on humans, on animals, on all forms of life. Where do you think the word 'lunatics' came from? Or the word 'loony-bin!' Need I say more! The moon pulls the waters in and out through the tides, and as our bodies are composed in large part of water, it certainly has an effect on us!

Native North American Indians referred to the moon and sun as 'Brother Sun, Sister Moon'. For them, the moon was a feminine, nurturing presence, very much a living, vital force in their lives. Their ceremonies and festivities were based around the moon and sun, and they understood the influence of all the planets on their spiritual development. Yes, the planets do affect us in their alignment, especially at the time of our birth. The nearest most of us get to believing this is in reading our 'stars' in the daily papers. But medieval people knew the importance of the planets and the power of their energies. Shakespeare's Romeo and Juliet, the *'star – crossed lovers',* and 'King Lear' – *'the stars make us what we are',* reflect medieval belief in the external energies that impact on our universe.

Today, belief in the spirits that surround us is strong. In India, Indonesia, South East Asia, South Pacific Islands, altars and shrines are common outside every dwelling, incense is regularly burned, offerings are placed, as an acknowledgement of the spirits guarding everything. In Bali, there are constant processions to the temples, women with flowers and fruit piled high on their heads, bringing the food to be blessed and brought home again to be shared among the family. In Vietnam and Cambodia, family shrines and burial plots are dotted across the land, encouraging the departed spirits to stay close to their families, protecting them and nurturing the land, helping the rice fields to produce abundantly, and keeping the animals safe. Departed souls have not gone anywhere; they are still a presence, looking after and protecting and nurturing their loved ones who are still on this dense earth vibrational frequency.

Chapter 8:

Holding us all together –
The interconnectedness of all things

We are not the only planet in our universe. Nor are we the only universe. There are millions upon trillions of stars and planets throughout all of the galaxies. And, as we have already seen, the Ancient Mystery Schools and the Ancients, Pythagoras in particular, thousands of years ago, all knew and taught that we are not just floating about in space at random, keeping our fingers crossed that we do not bump into each other. We are indeed held together through the most exquisite design, the most elaborate web of mathematics, sacred geometry and sound. A cacophony of sound, a great cosmic orchestral extravaganza, a harmonious blending of the vibrational energy frequencies constantly being emitted out into the ether by us and by all forms of life on this and all other planets, merging with the Great Universal God Energy Stream.

And within that Great Universal God Stream, we are all one. To quote the metaphysical poet John Donne again: *'No man is an island, entire of itself'*. There is no separateness. There is no disconnection from Divine Source, from each other, or from all the other forms of life with whom we share this wondrous planet. We are all united and connected, held together by the intricate, exquisite vast network of sacred cosmic geometry, the Metatron Cube, in the Infinite Energy Force that encompasses all that is, all that ever has been and all that ever will be, throughout the worlds, universes and galaxies in the entire cosmos, across all space and time, reaching into infinity, where time is non-existent, where past and future co-mingle and merge, manifesting in the present only.

This unifying Energy Force, as we have seen, omnipotent, omnipresent and omniscient, we call God, Great Spirit, Source, Divine Essence, the Light, whatever. It encompasses everything and we, as spiritual beings, and now at this point in time, incarnated as humans, are a spark of that Divine Essence, each connected to the other, woven together in the intricate web of the tapestry of life. We are inseparably connected to every form of life system with which, and with whom, we share this Planet Earth. We are here, not just to further our own individual ascension, but to enable the entire mass of humanity to ascend as well. Each and every soul is precious, and each and every precious soul must, and will, make its way eventually back to the Light, to Source, and we are all involved in that collective process. The responsibility lies on our shoulders, that is the reason after all why we are here, and why we will be returning for encore after encore, again and again and again, until all have been returned to the highest purest vibration of All That Is. Every form of life is connected. Plants, rocks, animals, rivers, oceans, sun, moon, rain — all of life, no matter what form it takes. We are all connected, sharing the vast wheel of spiritual energy.

Take the trees for example. They absorb the stale air we breathe out, transforming it into oxygen, which we in turn breathe in again in order to stay alive. The trees are the lungs of our precious earth. So part of me is in that tree. We are connected! The cloud in the sky becomes rain, which waters the soil that produces the food that I eat. So part of that cloud is in me. We are connected! Similarly, the sun grows everything I eat, nourishing and nurturing every living thing, so the sun is in me and I am part of the sun. We are connected! The house in which I live, the car I drive, the furniture I sit on, the clothes I wear, the television I watch – think of the long list of people involved in getting all those products produced and to me. The food on the supermarket shelves! The people who grow that food, all those who transported and packaged all that, those who made the transport that carried all that, those who built the transport network, those who supplied the fuel to move the transport. The list goes on, never ending.

Yes, we are all connected! I am you and you are me! I am the wind, I am the rain, I am the tree. As you too are! The only difference, as we saw earlier, is that we are all vibrating on different and various energy vibrational frequencies. The Native American Indians knew all about this. They knew, and lived their lives acknowledging that Great Spirit, the One Great Universal Energy Force is in all things. That is how they could simply raise a hand against the wind and make the wind die down. Or bring on the rain. Because they inherently knew, without any doubt whatsoever in their mind, that each one of them **was** the wind. So why could they not command the elements as they did? And modern day ***Shamans*** practise the same skills.

And we are not just connected spatially but also connected lineally, through all our ancestors, stretching back for aeons and down through our descendants, reaching into infinity. It is true that if a butterfly flaps its wings in South America, it affects the rest of the world. We are all in one great field of Divine Energy. What affects one affects all. Each and every action and thought causes a ripple or a domino effect throughout the entire network. Our thoughts and wishes go out into the ether as a form of energy and manifest somewhere in the Great Cosmic Dance. So be careful what you wish for! There are no straight lines in Nature! Everything is cyclical, coming round and round time and time again, into and beyond infinity.

When McCourt plays, the harmonious melody he sends out into the ether, harmonious because it is coming from his Higher Self, that higher energy vibrational frequency into which he is tuned as he composes and plays, then those sounds he emits through the piano, blend in with the great cosmic orchestral extravaganza and like everything else we send out, it all returns to us in an even more enhanced harmonious way, uplifting us, raising our own vibration, giving us that feel-good factor, sending us about our daily tasks with a lightness in our step, love in our heart and a deep knowing that we are tapped into something greater than us, something way beyond our physical sensory mechanism, beyond that which we experience through our limited five physical senses.

Chapter 9:

Getting into the Zone – raising our spiritual vibration

Creativity is within each one of us. It is the work of our soul and its realisation is necessary for our spiritual well-being. When we are realising and following our natural creative instincts, we are connecting with our soul, the very essence of ourselves. In order to allow our creative impulses to rise and to flourish, we need to connect with our soul, our Higher Self. Connecting with our own Higher Self is a pre-requisite for connecting with other energy frequency levels around us.

In order to connect with higher vibrational energies, with **All That Is,** we need to raise our own spiritual vibration. Then, and only then, can a connection be made.

Reiki and all other holistic practitioners need to raise their vibrational level in order to be able to channel healing energy. A connection needs to be made, and that connection can only be facilitated if a raise in consciousness takes place on the part of the practitioner. Holistic practitioners always use music in their therapy rooms. Even when meditating, the process of raising our vibrational frequency is enhanced through the meditation music we play.

And we have seen throughout this book that music is our gateway into these higher vibrational frequency levels. And it is through the great musical composers that we can get through that gateway.

They take us with them as they themselves access the higher vibrational frequencies.

But there is also another aspect to consider when trying to connect with other higher frequency energy levels. What are we putting into our bodies? Apart from smoking and drinking alcohol, and of course, filling our system with all sorts of medication and drugs, all keeping us in the dense vibrational energy frequency, we need to consider the food we eat.

Yes, the food we eat!

We simply just cannot make a clear connection to higher frequency energy levels if we are eating heavy energy, dense frequency foods. And our supermarket shelves are full of it! And not only there! We are surrounded by it. Food is everywhere. The food industry is the most lucrative world-wide.

Like all commercial ventures, the food industry is there to make money and what goes into the food chain is secondary to that prime concern. All farm animals are reared now for specifically one purpose, to be slaughtered for the food chain, and whatever food makes them fatter and more substantial, then that will be fed to them. All crops are grown now for one purpose, to enter the food chain. So whatever encourages them to grow more quickly, then that substance will be applied to them. We are soaking up into our system all the artificial chemical substances applied to the crops we eat. And we wonder why we have so much illness and disease in our world?

All animals die in trauma. They sense, they know, that death is imminent. They can smell the blood of the animal in front of them being killed. Have you ever noticed the heavy dense energy hanging around an abattoir?

Even fish die in trauma, either with a hook piercing their mouth, or caught in a net gasping for breath. And apart from that, of course, what is in our waters? What are we consuming?

And when we consume that flesh, we are soaking up part of that trauma. And again, we wonder why we have so much illness and disease in our world?

By eating and feeding such heavy density food into our bodies, we are keeping ourselves firmly stuck on the dense vibration on which most people continue to exist on this earthly plane.

Everything, including our food, is artificially processed. The farmer does not even touch the soil of Mother Earth any more. How different from our ancestors!

We regard the Native North American Indians as being very spiritual people, very much in touch with Mother Nature and with all things spiritual. And yes, they hunted and killed the buffalo! So what is the difference between them killing and eating the buffalo and we today killing animals for our food chain?

Well, for a start, the Native American Indian killed only when and as he needed food. Furthermore, each and every part of the buffalo was used. Nothing was wasted. The skin was used for their tepee covers, the sinews were used for thread, the hooves for cups and utensils, the tail for brushes, even the eyes had a use, for buttons. And out of respect for the soul of the animal, the heart was buried in the earth. The earth was their Mother and they respected it as such.

And it is that lack of respect for the earth and for Mother Nature that is so rampant in our world today. We subjugate and misuse free animals, for our pleasure and service, and not for their benefit. We use them and abuse them for sport, for mercenary means, for entertainment, and of course chiefly for food. And for food that we do not actually need to be eating!

In China, there are no dogs or cats in the streets. And why not? Simply because they are eaten. In fact, every year in China, there is a dog cookery festival. How obscene is that?

So, if we desire to raise our spiritual vibrational energy level, then we have got to pay attention to the type of food we are consuming. If we really do feel that we must eat meat, then at least we should thank the soul of the creature for sacrificing itself for our nourishment. But how many of us actually do even this?

If we consume dense energy foods, then we are keeping ourselves in the dense energy vibrational level. If we want to move above that dense vibrational energy to a higher vibrational level, then we have got to eat the higher vibrational foods, those foods which grow on trees or come out of the soil, with no added chemical substances. That's it in a nut shell!

And let us not forget what else keeps us stuck on the lower dense vibrational frequencies! Those feelings and thoughts we harbour as we go about our daily lives. The anger, the guilt, the fear, the lack of love, the spite, the jealousy, the greed, the desire for more and more.

And no musician, no matter how great a genius he may be, can get us into a higher vibrational frequency level if we are keeping ourselves stuck in heavy dense energy, unable to raise our own vibration. For the musician merely opens the door for us, he cannot pull us through. He is going through, but we cannot go with him, we cannot go through that beckoning door to the higher vibrational levels, if we are holding grudges, seething with anger, spite or jealousy, or intent on having, having, having, getting, getting, getting.

We will just get stuck in the doorway!

Chapter 10:

Cymatics, harmonious resonance and the Ancients

by Declan Quigley

In today's modern societies, we see ourselves as being extremely advanced in terms of technological development and use of technological advancements to enhance our contemporary lifestyles. Unfortunately, in many quarters, we look back towards the ancient peoples and regard them as simplistic and underdeveloped.

This couldn't be further from the truth! In fact, in some cultures, there appears to be a far more heightened understanding of certain technologies of which we in the modern age have only a rudimentary understanding.

For instance, as 21st Century people, we are only now getting a grasp on the wonderful attributes of music, sound, frequency and vibration. It would appear that sound was used quite extensively in ancient societies, to heal, to lift heavy objects and as a means by which our ancestors could connect with their Gods.

In fact, sound was the very fabric of creation for some ancient cultures and in many creation stories, sound is the active element in the creation of the World. For instance, one of the most prominent is found in the Holy Bible, where St. John proclaims, *"In the beginning was the Word and the Word was with God and the Word was God"* (John 1:1)

In the Hindu tradition, it is suggested that creation arose from the first sound of the Universe, 'Om'. This is a common belief in many of the Far Eastern religions, such as Buddhism and Shintoism. Both the God Shiva and the God Vishnu used a conch shell and a drum to create this sound, stimulating the birth and growth of the World.

For the ancient Egyptians, there was the belief that Thoth and Ma'at created the World though chanting a single word. The Mayan people of Central America also had a similar belief. In the North American Hopi Nation, they told the tale of the *'Spider Woman',* who sang the World into being.

To us, in modern times, routed in Newtonian physics, these stories may seem implausible. However, recent research by Dr. Hans Jenny, (1967) on Cymatics, the study of the effect of sound waves on matter, highlights that specific tones, properly directed, can not only organise matter, known as micro-sonic scaffolding, but indeed, can create material geometric form, similar to microscopic life.

In similar research, Vicktor Schauberger, suggested that sound can create micro-vortexes in water. This phenomenon may be responsible for assembling the essential components for the creation of DNA. (Bartholomew, 2004)

The ancients also believed that they could connect with their deities through the use of sound and did indeed, create temples, buildings and structures to manifest and promote certain frequencies, allowing themselves access to their Gods.

There is much evidence to suggest that many sacred sites, stone circles and temples have been structured to enable '*harmonic resonance*' in certain frequencies and to illicit certain tones, ultimately to create particular states of mind.

In Chichen Itza, Mexico, at the site of 'La Castilla' pyramid, it was found that the ancient Mayan 'ballcourt' was structured in such a way that distance did not minimise the sound of the human voice. The effect is that someone speaking in a low tone can be very clearly and audibly heard over the distance of the 'ballcourt', which was five hundred and forty five feet.

Also at La Castilla, it was found that the sound of a single hand clap resonating around the pyramid, when measured with a sonogram, creates a near perfect imitation of the cry of the Quetzal bird, a sacred power animal of the Mayan people and the bird dedicated to the God that the pyramid was built to honor, Quetzalcoatl.

In the Great Pyramid at Giza, Egypt, it is known that the ancient Egyptians would chant within the 'King's Chamber', the purpose of which was to connect with their Gods. An unusual phenomenon, found in the Great Pyramid and many other sacred sites around the world is a perfect harmonic resonance between 90hz and 120hz, which is approximately the frequency of a low male voice.

This has also been found at the temple complex at Angkor Wat in Cambodia, the Hypogeum in Malta and at Newgrange and other passage tombs in Ireland, with a common resonance of 111hz. In one Irish mythological story, relating to the Cave of the Cats at Rathcroghan in Co. Roscommon, it is documented that access to the 'Otherworld' of Spirit could be gained by using a low male voice (approx.. 110hz) to open a portal.

Paul Devereaux and Jahn et al (1996) have carried out extensive research into what is becoming known as *'archaeo-acoustics',* the study of sound at archaeological sites. They discovered that this frequency of 111hz is a common phenomenon in hundreds of sacred sites around the world.

So, why such a specific frequency? Cook et al (2008) suggest that this particular frequency of approximately 110hz, excites certain areas of the brain that are commonly highlighted in deep and intense meditation.

During clinical conditions, it was found that, when this frequency was played to subjects, there was a very obvious switch in electrical activity from the left temporal region of the brain to the right temporal region.

Activity in this area of the brain has been linked to emotional processing, self awareness, psychic abilities and higher insight. This would give some credence to the supposition that the ancients were using sound frequency in an attempt to connect psychically to their Gods.

Clearly the ancient peoples had a profound knowledge of acoustics and frequency and how to structure their environments in such a way as to use this to its greatest potential. In many mythological tales, it is suggested that certain sacred sites, or temples, were built by levitating huge stone boulders into place through the use of sound.

In certain accounts of the building of Stonehenge, it is documented that the wizard Merlin, using sound, levitated the huge stones from a quarry in Wales, hundreds of miles to the site of Stonehenge.

In the tales of the ancient Bolivian Shaman, it is said that the huge precision cut stones that comprise the sacred site of Pumapunku at Tiahuanacu were levitated into place at the request of their light-skinned, red-haired God, Viracocha.

To many, this may seem fairly far-fetched! However, if you consider that at the University of Bristol, they have recently discovered that certain acoustic frequencies can indeed levitate very small objects and droplets of water (Marzo et al, 2017), it is strongly felt that with a little more research, larger objects will indeed be levitated through sonic means.

The ancient indigenous Shamanic communities throughout the world had a profound understanding of the benefit of healing through sound and vibration. Shamans used many sound based techniques, such as drumming and rattling to create altered states of consciousness, placing them in a '*Spiritual landscape*', where they could meet their Helping Spirits and Spiritual Guides.

However, in recent times, the use of sound to heal has grown in prominence, also mirroring ancient Shamanic understanding. Research has discovered that there is indeed a curative effect to sound, frequency and vibration.

Fundamentally, drumming rhythm was our first music and creative expression, mimicking the heart beat in the womb. The ancient Shamans were also acutely aware that there was a further purpose, a healing purpose, to their rhythms.

In the modern day, there is emphasis placed on the physiological and psychological effects of drumming and how this can bring significant balance and regeneration to the body.

For instance, much research has been carried out on how drumming can clear emotional blockages, allowing release to take place, without medication. This has been found to be successful when addressing addictions, depression and anxiety.

Drumming has also been proven to have a therapeutic effect in dealing with trauma. Lawrence Friedman, in *'The Healing Power of the Drum',* (2000) states that the effect of a drum sound can diminish stress and anxiety, high blood pressure and fight depression.

It is also being discovered that this natural rhythmic approach can have a therapeutic effect on the immune system, increasing the flow of natural analgesics and even having a positive effect with cancer patients. Cancer specialist, Dr. Barry Bittman states that, *"drumming tunes our biology, orchestrates our immunity, and enables healing to begin."* (Bittman et al, 2001)

Also, in cases of Alzheimers, MS, Autism and Stroke patients, it has been found that drumming promotes their ability to interact on a more positive level. Their cognitive ability was also seen to improve. (Friedman, 1994)

The theoretical basis for healing through sound is that all matter vibrates at a specific frequency which can both influence and be influenced by all other vibrations (Gaynor, 1999; Roosth, 2009). Gerber, (1998) found that there was a cranial nerve that connects the eardrum to every organ in the human body, except the spleen, allowing a healing effect to take place throughout the body. (Gerber, 1998).

The theory behind this is that by subjecting patients to various frequencies, healers harmonize cells, organs, and biological systems which may have been disrupted, blocked, or out of synchronisation with the remainder of the body and its environment.

Dr. Monroe, of the Monroe Institute, had similar results with the application of conflicting tones played though headphones to the patient, *'Binaurel Beats'*, one tone played in each ear. This was found to have had significant results, having the effect of balancing both hemispheres of the brain.

Under this principle, there are two main theories detailing how sound can facilitate healing. Firstly, when a structure such as a human organ vibrates at a frequency that is not harmonious with the total bodily frequency, it does not absorb positive energy as efficiently and becomes susceptible to disease. Therefore, the introduction of the organ's natural frequency will have a modelling and healing effect on the diseased part of the body. (Crowe & Scovel, 1996).

Secondly, the vibrations of the sound wave may aid the natural flow of substances transported through the cell wall and the excretion of waste products out through the cell wall. (Keyhani et al., 2001; Yount et al., 2004).

Dr. Peter Guy Manners (1940) suggested that our body and our organs have a natural resonant frequency, or *'bio-signature'*. When our organs become diseased they lose this particular frequency. It is the clinician's task then to create balance and restore the body's natural frequency, thus promoting good health.

An important area of new medical research into the health properties of sound is centred around the use of sound outside the range of normal human hearing. For many years, ultrasound has been used for the imaging, diagnosing, and treatment of many conditions

First developed during the Second World War, ultrasound devices offer both diagnostic and therapeutic properties by emitting an oscillating sound pressure wave at frequencies above the hearing range of humans. Ultrasound is now proving an effective tool in combating pain associated with arthritis, scar tissue and other conditions.

Don Campbell (2001) also discovered that playing the music of Mozart had a profound effect on the brain capacity, spatial awareness and attention of students when studying or answering questions. Much research has also been devoted to '*bio-sonics*', the study of the effect of sound, particularly Mozart on growing organisms such as plants. This has been found to yield some very exciting results, especially when the plant is placed under certain geometric structures such as pyramids.

Dr. A. Tomatis (1991) observed that what we hear has a significant effect on our bodily health. Whilst studying the behaviour of Benedictine Monks, he observed that following a period of abstinence from their usual chanting, most fell ill. When the chanting regime was reinstated, their health took a dramatic change for the better.

Music of the Spheres

The use of certain frequencies found in sacred music, particularly Gregorian Chants, most notably used by the Benedictine Order, have been found to improve overall physical, emotional and psychological health. These notes have become known as the *'Solfeggio Frequencies'*.

Solfeggio Frequencies make up the ancient six tone scale thought to have been used in ancient Spiritual music, including the beautiful and well known Gregorian Chants. The chants and their special tones were believed to interact with the body's energetic system through the chakras when sung in harmony.

Each tone corresponds to a given chakra and the energetic significance of that chakra. When played, this balances and returns the chakra to optimum frequency and optimum performance.

The six original Solfeggio Frequencies and their healing focus are described below:

396 Hz – Liberating Guilt and Fear

417 Hz – Undoing Situations and Facilitating Change

528 Hz – Transformation and Miracles (DNA Repair)

639 Hz – Connecting/Relationships

741 Hz – Expression/Solutions

852 Hz – Returning to Spiritual Order

Prof. Willi Apel, (1944) states that the Solfeggio Scale was first found in the medieval hymn to John the Baptist, *'Ut Queant Laxis'* and developed by a Benedictine Monk, Guido d'Arezzo. The construction of the hymn was that the first six lines commenced respectively on the first six successive notes of the scale.

Therefore, the first syllable of each line was one degree higher than the first syllable of the line that preceded it. Today, we know the Solfeggio Scale as seven ascending notes assigned to the syllables Do-Re-Mi-Fa-So-La-Ti. The original scale however, was six ascending notes assigned to Ut-Re-Mi-Fa-Sol-La.

Nikola Tesla, stated that, *"If you only knew the magnificence of the 3, 6 and 9, then you would hold a key to the universe"*. The 3, 6, and 9 are the fundamental root vibrations of the Solfeggio Frequencies. It has been suggested that the implicit beauty of the Solfeggio Frequencies are that they bring you back into balance with Source, the healing music of the heavenly spheres and the Universe

The use of the Solfeggio Frequencies has been found to be a significant insight into the workings of the body's energetic system and an extremely effective healing method. However, the impact of the Solfeggio Frequencies in modern music has been significantly diminished since modern musical standard tuning has changed.

This issue has proved to be extremely controversial for many Spiritual practitioners, in that there is the feeling that musical standard tuning was changed from the Spiritually uplifting A=444Hz, to a more discordant and un-Spiritual A=440Hz. This was changed at the insistence of the BBC in 1939, who suggested that the A=440Hz tuning was much more appropriate for radio broadcast.

There are those who would suggest that during that era, the Rothschilds and Rockefeller families were in control of World media organisations such as the BBC and changing standard tuning was a means by which this cabal could undermine healing and Spiritual *'upliftment'* for the population.

When used along with specific frequencies, the addition of personal intention cannot be under-estimated. When this is used, the opportunity for a positive healing outcome is intensified. Intention consists of using your focused thoughts, feelings and visualizations to attract the desired outcome.

Dr. Stephen Halpern states that *'Sound is a carrier wave of consciousness. One's intention is the spiritual counterpart of the sound and the combination of sound and intention create the outcome of healing'*.

Jonathan Goldman, (1992) created this simple formula: *Sound + Intention = Healing.* Similarly, when working as chief psychiatrist at Hawaii State Mental Hospital, Dr. Hew Linn combined his healing intention with the ancient Hawaiian chant of *'Ho'oponopono,'* whilst reviewing the medical records of the inmates. In a matter of months, the number of inmates in the hospital had diminished by at least 75%.

In his book, *'The Spontaneous Healing of Belief'* (2007), author Gregg Braden described how he witnessed a woman with advanced cancer being cured by the doctors in a *'medicineless'* hospital in China.

In a matter of moments, the doctors simply chanted a phrase that was similar to, *'already done'*, suggesting that the cure had already happened. He watched the tumour on a CCTV screen and was amazed as the tumour completely disappeared.

The use of sound in our modern societies appears to be very much in its infancy in regards to its many applications. This is a field of interest in which we cannot conceive the positive, long term benefits of research and investment. We see specifically, however, that there are huge implications for medical practitioners when prescribing heavy duty pharmaceuticals. This, in itself may save millions of lives.

Undoubtedly, this could have the effect of, at last, freeing patients from the negative contra-indications of these toxic and poisonous chemicals and, of course, the stranglehold of the pharmaceutical companies, not only on the medical profession, but on our governments and law-makers.

The field of health aside, research and development of sound in many walks of life can only be hugely beneficial to our societies. Not least amongst these is a means by which to enhance and extend our personal Spirituality, to effectively connect with Source, or Universal intelligence. And perhaps, finally, to return, in some ways to the balance and natural wisdom of our ancient ancestors and the technological understandings that are so absent in our supposedly advanced world.

Declan Quigley. 2018.

References:

Bartholomew, Alick (2004) Hidden Nature: The Startling Insights of Vicktor Schauberger. Floris Books

Braden. Gregg, (2007) The Spontaneous Healing of Belief. Hay House

Campbell, Don. (2001) The Mozart Effect: Tapping the Power of Music to Heal the Body, Strengthen the Mind, and Unlock the Creative Spirit. New York: Harper Paperbacks, 2001.

Cook, Ian A.; Pajot, Sarah K.; Leuchter, Andrew F., (2008) "Ancient Architectural Acoustic Resonance Patterns and Regional Brain Activity," Time and Mind, Volume 1, Number 1,

Devereaux, Paul. (2001) Stone Age Soundtracks. Vega Books

Devereux, Paul, et al (2001) "Acoustical Properties of Ancient Ceremonial Sites," Journal of Scientific Exploration, 9:438,

Friedman, L. (2000) The Healing Power of the Drum. White Cliffs Media Co.

Goldman. J, (1992) Healing Sounds: The Power of Harmonics. Healing Sounds Books.

Jahn, Robert G., et al; (1995) "Acoustical Resonances of Assorted Ancient Structures," Technical Report PEAR 95002, Princeton University,

Jenny, Hans. (2001) Cymatics: A Study of Wave Phenomenon and

Vibration. Macromedia Publishing

Marzo, A. Barnes, A. and B.W. Drinkwater, (2017) TinyLev: A multi-emitter single-axis acoustic levitator'. Review of Scientific Instruments. University of Bristol

Quigley, D. (2017) Intermediate Module Three: Healing with Sound and Frequency. Shamanic Practitioner's Course. The Irish School of Shamanic Studies.

Tomatis, A. A. The Conscious Ear: My Life of Transformation Through Listening. Station Hill Press, 1991.

Declan Quigley is an Irish Shamanic Practitioner, Healer, Tutor, Writer and Founder of Anam Nasca Shamanism Ireland. He runs workshops, training events and healing clinics throughout Ireland. For further information, contact Declan on anamnasca@gmail.com, or on Facebook, Twitter and Instagram.

Chapter 11:

Music and the body and soul

There is more to music than meets the ear! Much more than just octaves, crotchets, quavers, semibreves, sharps, flats, allegros and crescendos.

Pythagoras taught that music should never be seen simply as a form of entertainment or pleasure. Rather, he recognized that music was an expression of *'harmonia',* the divine and universal principle that brings order to chaos and disorder. As such, through music, man was able to see into the structure of nature and life. And furthermore, if used correctly, Pythagoras taught, music can bring the faculties of the soul into harmony with these structures, composing and purifying the mind and body, and thus restoring and maintaining perfect health.

Pythagoras himself used music in all his healings. He was able to identify specific states of mind and the particular rhythms and melodies that had produced them, and then, likewise, he could identify the specific rhythms and melodies that would counteract or reverse them. Thus he was able to heal people of passions such as anger, despair, sorrow, envy, jealousy or pride. He also advocated certain forms of body and dance movement to cure such short-comings or ailments, accompanied by the eight-stringed lyre.

Pythagoras fed his followers a session of music each evening before they retired, blending particular intervals and various modulations of his voice into melodies designed to free them from the stress and strain of the day. These evening songs induced a restful sleep for those who heard them. Likewise, each morning, they were awakened to the sound of specially designed rhythms, tones and voice modulations, this time in order to stimulate them and set them up for the day ahead. He also advocated different melodies and combinations for each season.

Pythagoras, in his understanding of the power and significance of universal harmonies, including the harmonious sounds made by the planets as they continued on their orbital path, and able to hear them because of what he claimed to be his acute and extraordinary sense of hearing, was then in turn able to reproduce these same sounds through his own voice modulations or through various musical instruments. Through working out musical notes as a progressive series of octaves, Pythagoras was ultimately able to translate all the fundamental principles of the universe which he discovered into the language of mathematics and music. Thus he was able to demonstrate to his disciples the harmony of the universe, and how the health of the body was also dependent on the harmony within the human body itself.

For the Pythagoreans, mathematics and music were everything. Within the principle of Mathematics, Arithmetic was the study of quantity; geometry dealt with static three-dimensional forms; astronomy was concerned with bodies when in motion and undergoing change, and music identified the relationship between quantities. The beauty of the stars and the planets lay in their specific arrangement to each other and the order in which they revolved, the entire heavens illustrating the sublime wisdom that resulted only from structure, and complete harmony instilled from divine perfection through numbers, perfect figures and relationships.

Harmony or harmonic relations underlie all of Pythagoras' teachings, the *'harmonia'* of the Spheres, the *'harmonia'* of all creation. This Pythagorean conception of the universe as a musical-numerical system rapidly became the standard throughout the Mediterranean world. Music has been a part of every aspect of spirituality in all cultures throughout the world, whether that is religious or an innate sense of spirituality. Ancient as well as modern religious practices have incorporated sound, music and rhythm into their rituals of worship and spirituality.

There is no doubt that down through history and in our modern world, the importance of music and the significant effects music has on the human mind and body is clearly understood and utilized. And like everything else, there are always those who will abuse and misuse whatever is available to them in their greed for power and money. And somewhere along the line, music, like everything else, was hijacked and used for less than worthy purposes, the original intent being distorted and thwarted.

We have music playing constantly around us, much of it manipulating us into certain thought patterns or action. Music is a conductor for certain types of energies, most obviously for emotions, transferring the emotions of the music composer or creator to the emotions of the listener. Less obviously, music is a conductor of intent, transferring the consciousness of the music creator to the consciousness of the listener.

For example, in a doctor's or dentist's waiting room, the music is specially designed to pacify us and keep us calm. At an award giving ceremony, it is the direct opposite, the music hyped up as we go on stage. Likewise in a sports gym, the hyped-up music is specially designed to get us moving our bodies. Wedding music is different from that chosen for funerals, each specifically geared toward inducing particular emotions in us. Major sports events and games begin and end with the National Anthem, meant to induce feelings of nationalism, togetherness and pride in our country.

Hitler certainly knew the strength and power of this use of music! His huge nationalist rallies were always accompanied by loud, robust music and marching songs, suggestive of strength and power, and instilling pride for the Fatherland into the German people. And he certainly exemplified the ancient Greeks in their supposition that music can be used for evil purposes as well as for positive outcomes. Before his appearances in front of the crowds at his massive rallies, music was already playing, building the crowd up to fever pitch. Then he would appear, the mad thunderous cheering drowning out the music, which had now done its job of heightening emotions, ensuring that those heightening emotions all peaked simultaneously, an accomplished feat so dangerously characteristic of large crowd behaviour. His rhetoric would then take on a quality of incantation or chant, making little sense in the fact that no information was imparted through his words. But he mesmerised the crowds in front of him. He put a spell on them, transfixing them, hypnotising them, arousing them, using words to reinforce the effect which the music, the banners, the loudspeakers, the placards had already fostered in them. Even though his voice was harsh and unmusical, he managed to strike the right chord with them by exploiting the basic human need to belong, to be part of a social group, to be part of a unified country. And why? Why, despite the harshness of his voice, and that rasping sound that he emitted, so unpleasant to the ear, did he manage to control them so completely? Why was he so able to sweep huge crowds of people off their feet just by his words, which often did not make any sense?

Simply because he understood the importance and significance of music as a powerful weapon in the hands of any fanatic. And it was not just the words. Hitler *chanted his words in a sort of monotonous incantation.* And this was how he was able to overwhelm people emotionally. This and his use of language as it is used in religious ritual. All meant to overpower the listener and suspend any sort of rational thinking in his mind, surrendering himself to the emotional power of the moment. Yes, Hitler was a clever guy! He had it all worked out!

As had Winston Churchill. The rasping, unmusical voice, but all delivered in a sort of musical chanting, a monotonous though rhythmic incantation, as for example in his famous '*We will fight them on the beaches*' speech.

And today, advertising companies also utilize the power of music, in their case, to persuade us to buy. Telephone services no less recognise the value of music, when we are left hanging on at the other end of the line, the particular music chosen to pacify and calm us down in the midst of our irritation.

Note too, the power of such maestros as Andre Rieu! He has his audience crying, laughing, dancing, pleading for more, at one minute quiet and the next boisterous. Elvis Presley too played his audiences, raising them up, lowering them in order to raise them up again. All these musicians and performers know it has all got to with the energy generated by music and the vibrational energy frequencies on which they send the music out.

Music helps purge anger, pain, and all forms of emotional upsets. There are in fact very few stimuli that are able to induce as intense emotional experiences as music. Music is played in schools, in art classes or any hands-on activities, where it acts as a creative stimulus, connecting the listener to the creative forces flowing through to him from his Higher Self, reaching far beyond the mind and into the deep subconscious, the overall aim being to find one's spiritual center in expressing oneself.

Music can enable brain-damaged people to accomplish tasks beyond their natural ability. Children and adults with learning difficulties can be helped through music. Mentally ill or emotionally disturbed people respond to music. *But not just any music.* In order to help such people, the music must resonate with them, and in resonating with them, it makes structured sense of the world around them, bringing a feeling of stability and calmness to their troubled mind. And that sense of structure and calmness comes from the musician.

Six pianists indeed could play the same melody, and each would have a different effect on the listener. And why? Again, it has got to do with the energy vibrational frequency of the musician! The vibration comes from within the composer, out to the external world of physical vibration and is picked up by the listener. So the musician is, in essence, an instrument being played by God, as indeed we all are instruments of God, being played out in this Earth plane.

Music transcends religion, politics, race and nationality. It is the language of the soul, a spiritual medium, connecting us to those other spirit realms, to the cosmos and to entire creation.

Spirit is breath, breath is Spirit. Breath is the transmitter of Spirit. When we pass over at the end of each physical life, our Spirit departs our body with our last breath. When the Reiki Master attunes a student to the Reiki healing energy modality, the sacred symbols are blown into the student's crown chakra through the breath. Music helps us to relax, and therefore breathe more deeply, facilitating our process of connecting with Spirit. Our breathing helps us become congruent with the Great Universal Energy Field, and it is then that the divine flows through us.

Music is indeed the foundation stone within each life form. And because the whole world is made up of sound and rhythm, playing or listening to music connects us to the all pervasive powers in our universe.

Abba summed it all up neatly:

'So I say

Thank you for the music, the songs I'm singing

Thanks for all the joy they're bringing

Who can live without it, I ask in all honesty

What would life be?

Eileen McCourt

Without a song or a dance what are we?

So I say thank you for the music

For giving it to me'

Chapter 12:

The Musicality and Spirituality of William Butler Yeats

William Butler Yeats was born in Dublin in 1865, into a wealthy County Sligo family, who later returned to live in County Sligo, where his great-grand father had been rector of the Parish Church in Drumcliff, where Yeats is buried. Yeats' great-great-grandfather had, in 1773, married Mary Butler, of a landed family in Co. Kildare, and the name Butler was thereafter kept in the family name. They were descendants of the first Earls of Ormond.

It was the area around Sligo that the young poet came to think of as his childhood and spiritual home. Its landscape and its location on the sea became, over time, both literally and symbolically, his *country of the heart*.

Yeats' childhood and young adulthood were shadowed by the power shift away from the minority Protestant Ascendancy in Ireland and the momentum of nationalism, all of which had a profound effect on his poetry.

Spirituality, as we have seen throughout this book, is all about connecting with what lies beyond our five physical senses. It is a desire, a deep longing, a search to find and to appreciate more than we can see and hear in what we believe to be our natural reality. It is a strong yearning for a deep connection to our inherent divine spiritual essence.

We have seen too that our spiritual essence, call it our soul, our spirit, is the pure God essence that we carry within us, the pure God essence that each of us is. And our God essence, our Soul, is connected to the Great Universal God Energy, the Great Universal Consciousness, outside of which, nothing and no-one can possibly have any sort of existence.

All the great sages, musicians, writers, poets, they all knew this. The great metaphysical poet of the middle ages, John Donne, the great Romantic poets, Wordsworth, Coleridge, Blake, and of course, our own William Butler Yeats and William Percy French. They all knew, we are all connected, we are all one, in the great web of connectedness, And they knew too, we are not alone. These people had the ability to tap into other higher energy vibrational frequencies that constantly surround us on all sides.

William Butler Yeats was indeed what we call a '*shaman*'. The shamanic practitioner is an energy frequency and vibrational specialist. Shamanism is not a religion. It transcends religion. Shamanic practitioners in general, hold an '*animistic*' view, that everything is energy and these energies are all held in a central grid. It can be said that this grid is God or Source or the Great Universal Consciousness, or whatever the perspective of the practitioner. By means of the '*shamanic journey*', we are connecting into this massive grid of Godliness.

Native American Indians were of course shamans, and very powerful shamans at that. But shamanism is by no means exclusive to Native North American Indians.

Irish Literature is permeated with references to the shamanic journey throughout the ages. Most notable would be the tales of the Tuatha De Dannan, the Formorians, the Milesians, CuChullain of Ulster and Queen Maeve. Then we have the stories of, for example, the Children of Lir, which highlights the shamanic tradition of *'shape-shifting',* or Oisin in Tir Na N'Og, another typical example of a shamanic journey.

The Celtic tales of England, Scotland and Wales also have this very same cultural tradition of heroes who *'journey'* to the *'Otherworld'* in search of healing, knowledge or power for their community. The Tales of King Arthur, the Knights of the Round Table and Merlin are some of the most famous Celtic tales to involve the shamanic journey. King Arthur's journey to Annwn, the Underworld of the British Celts, to find the Cauldron of Inspiration and Rebirth, is a Celtic Otherworld journey. In the Welsh tradition, Arthur is accompanied on these journeys by a shaman by the name of Taliesin. In more recent scholarly and radical volumes. it has, in fact, been suggested that the pre-Celtic civilizations of Ireland, Scotland, England and Wales, originated from the island of Atlantis. They went on to inform the rest of the world in relation to the core Shamanic, Spiritual and social practices through the druidic colleges that were established throughout the world. (*Declan Quigley, from his Irish School of Shamanic Studies practitioner manual. Declan is co-founder of the Irish School of Shamanic Studies and founder of the Anam Nasca Shamanism Ireland*)

The poems of William Butler Yeats are rich in shamanic imagery and philosophy. Perhaps the best-known of such is his *'Song of Wandering Aengus'.*

Eileen McCourt

This work was inspired by and based on the legend of the Gaelic love God Aengus. In the legend, Aengus is awakened out of his sleep by the vision of an amazingly beautiful woman. He becomes obsessed by her beauty and takes off wandering (*Wandering Aengus*) in search of her, hungering for her love. He finally discovers her at a lake, where she has been changed by magic into a swan.

The message coming from Yeats' poem is that one can spend an entire life-time chasing after a dream. It is the journey that is important, and not so much actually achieving the dream. One must keep on being motivated, curious and desiring in life. Notice in the first two stanzas there is the mention of fire. The motivation for the speaker is the fire in his head, leading him on. The hazel wand as a fishing rod and the berry hooked to a thread are the means of achieving the dream. Then, despite him kindling a fire, the silver trout turns into a girl with '*apple blossoms*' in her hair. So on he wanders again. In the final stanze, he is '*old with wandering*' and still has not managed to catch up with her. The '*silver apples of the moon,* the *golden apples of the sun*' are no doubt symbolic of the fruition of the dream.

Music of the Spheres

'I went out into the hazel wood,

Because a fire was in my head,

And cut and peeled a hazel wand,

And hooked a berry to a thread;

And when white moths were on the wing,

And moth-like stars were flickering out,

I dropped the berry in a stream

And caught a little silver trout.

When I had laid it on the floor

I went to blow the fire a-flame,

But something rustled on the floor,

And someone called me by my name:

It had become a glimmering girl

With apple blossom in her hair

Who called me by my name and ran

And faded through the brightening air.

Eileen McCourt

Though I am old with wandering

Through hollow lands and hilly lands,

I will find out where she has gone,

And kiss her lips and take her hands;

And walk among long dappled grass,

And pluck till time and times are done,

The silver apples of the moon,

The golden apples of the sun.'

In another of Yeats' poems, '*The Stolen Child*', we see Yeats' belief in other vibrational frequencies all around us. Call them the fairies, the little folk, whatever, but our ancestors were much more tuned into their subtle, pervasive, but non-invasive presence. It was believed that now and then the fairies would steal away a human child and replace it with a fairy child, a '*changeling*' in order to infiltrate the human ranks.

Music of the Spheres

¹*Where dips the rocky highland*

Of Sleuth Woods in the lake,

There lies a leafy island

Where flapping herons wake

The drowsy water rats;

There we've hid our faery vats,

Full of berrys

And of reddest stolen cherries.

Come away, O human child!

To the waters and the wild

With a faery, hand in hand,

For the world's more full of weeping than you can understand.

Where the wave of moonlight glosses

The dim gray sands with light,

Far off by furthest Rosses

We foot it all the night,

Weaving olden dances

Mingling hands and mingling glances

Eileen McCourt

Till the moon has taken flight;

To and fro we leap

And chase the frothy bubbles,

While the world is full of troubles

And anxious in its sleep.

Come away, O human child!

To the waters and the wild

With a faery, hand in hand,

For the world's more full of weeping than you can understand.

Where the wandering water gushes

From the hills above Glen-Car,

In pools among the rushes

That scarce can bathe a star,

We seek for slumbering trout

And whispering in their ears

Give them unquiet dreams;

Leaning softly out

From ferns that drop their tears

Music of the Spheres

Over the young streams.

Come away, O human child!

To the waters and the wild

With a faery, hand in hand,

For the world's more full of weeping than you can understand.

Away with us he's going,

The solemn-eyed:

He'll hear no more the lowing

Of the calves on the warm hillside

Or the kettle on the hob

Sing peace into its breast,

Or see the brown mice bob

Round and round the oatmeal chest.

For he comes, the human child,

To the waters and the wild

With a faery, hand in hand,

For the world's more full of weeping than he can understand.'

William Butler Yeats was not a composer of music or song. His creativity was expressed in his poetry. That does not mean that there was no musicality in his works. There is musicality in all poetry, as there is in all words and language. There may not be a musical instrument accompanying, or it may not be sung, but it is still, as we have seen throughout this book, a frequency, a vibration, like absolutely everything else. There is a musicality and rhythm in everything. Rhythm is frequency, frequency is vibration, vibration is everything.

The musicality of Yeats' work comes through nowhere more clearly than in his famous poem, *'Lake Isle of Innisfree'*. Yeats is living in London, in the hustle and bustle of the busy streets, and yearning for the peace and solitude of his beloved County Sligo and the Island of Innisfree. The poem reflects the desire of the shaman for solitude and quiet where the soul can connect with the higher Intelligence, the Great Universal God Consciousness.

Yeats brings out the musicality through his unique combination of vowel sounds. Note how he starts off with the repetition of the vowel 'i': *'I will arise'*; then he changes to the 'o' vowel, *'and go now, and go to'*, and then returns to the 'i' sound, *'Innisfree'*. Next he incorporates an extended 'a' vowel sound, in *'and a small cabin build there of clay and wattles made'*. So as we can see, it is this combination of vowel sounds that gives this famous poem its musicality and rhythm.

Music of the Spheres

'I will arise and go now, and go to Innisfree,

And a small cabin build there, of clay and wattles made:

Nine bean rows will I have there, a hive for the honey-bee,

And live alone in the bee-loud glade.

And I shall have some peace there, for peace comes dropping slow,

Dropping from the veils of the morning to where the cricket sings.

There midnight's all a glimmer, and noon a purple glow,

And evening full of the linnet's wings.

I will arise and go now, for always night and day

I hear lake water lapping with low sounds by the shore;

While I stand on the roadway, or on the pavements grey,

I hear it in the deep heart's core.

Now compare the rhythm in '*Lake Isle of Innisfree*' to the rhythm and the musical beat in another of Yeats' poems, '*The Fiddler of Dooney*'.

Dooney Rock is located just outside Sligo itself, and has been immortalised in the prestigious instrumentalist competition held in Sligo at the Fiddler of Dooney Competition.

Eileen McCourt

'When I play on my fiddle in Dooney,

Folk dance like a wave of the sea;

My cousin is priest in Kilvarnet,

My brother in Mocharabuiee.

I passed my brother and cousin:

They read in their books of prayer;

I read in my book of songs

I bought at the Sligo fair.

When we come at the end of time

To Peter sitting in state,

He will smile on three old spirits,

But call me first through the gate;

For the good are always the merry,

Save by an evil chance,

And the merry love the fiddle,

And the merry love to dance:

Music of the Spheres

And when the folk there spy me,

They will all come up to me,

With 'Here is the fiddler of Dooney!'

And dance like a wave of the sea.'

Surely this sums up William Butler Yeats! While others read their prayer books, he reads his *'book of songs'*. And *'the good are always the merry'*, and *'the merry love the fiddle'*, and *'the merry love to dance'*.

There is a musicality in all poetry, as there is in all words and language. The Irish language itself is probably one of the most musical languages in the world today. Brian Friel's play *'Translations'* emphasises this very clearly. It is through the poetic sound of the place names and the musical tone to them that Maire and Yolland find a way to communicate their affection for each other. Yolland has fallen in love, not only with Maire, but also with the Irish language itself. The play illustrates how the musicality of the Irish place-names was lost when they were translated into English. For example, *'Baile Beag'* was translated into *'Ballybeg'*, *'Poll na gCaorach'* became *'the hole of the sheep'*, *'Ceann Balor'* was changed into *'head of Balor'*, *'Machaire Buidhe'* became *'yellow plane'*, *'Druim Dubh'* became *'black ridge'*, *'Bun na hAbhann'* became *'mouth of the river'* and *'Lis na Muc '* became the *'fort of the pigs'*.

See how the whole musicality got lost in the literal translation?

It is indeed the sound of the Gaelic place names that gives the whole play its poetic tone. Yolland and Maire pick up on the vowels of the names. When Yolland says '*Lis na nGall*', Maire follows with '*Lis na nGradh*'. By the repitition of '*Lis*' and the '*nG*' sound, a rhythm is created. They continue by repeating '*carraig*', '*loch*', '*machaire*' and '*cnoc*'.

And the musicality is also clear in such phrases as '*That's the point, you donkey you!*', '*Still footering about in the hedge*', '*Will you shut up, you aul eejit you!*' '*He's been on the batter since this morning*'.

So musicality is in all words, and all languages are composed of words. Musicality is in everything.

Pat McCourt has put several of William Butler Yeats' poems to music, enhancing even further the musicality already there, and capturing brilliantly and sensitively the mood of Yeats in each. For example, in '*The Stolen Child*', Pat has created a very light airy tone, reflective of fairies and waterfalls and children's laughter, compared to the much more sombre tone he has created in '*Lake Isle of Innisfree*', where the mood of Yeats is sad, melancholy and nostalgic, with a deep yearning in his being for the peace and quiet for which his soul constantly hungers.

And as we listen to Pat play his own compositions for Yeats' work, we too are linked into the Spirituality of William Butler Yeats, and through him, into the Great Universal Energy, The Great Universal Consciousness, All That Is, as we ourselves join in the Music of the Spheres.

Chapter 13:

The Musicality and Spirituality of William Percy French

Just as William Butler Yeats secured a place in our hearts with his poetry and the musicality of his poetry, so too William Percy French has secured his place, not only with his poetry, but also wth his delightfully enchanting songs and melodies. William Percy French is indeed, surely one of Ireland's literary greats.

Songwriter, musician, poet, watercolour artist, journalist, performer and entertainer, his travelling variety shows delighting countless audiences, from royalty to small gatherings in the halls of rural Ireland, with his trade mark comedy,- farce, parody and humour. His life and times have been well documented by Berrie O'Neill in his sensitively written and beautifully illustrated biography *'Tones That Are Tender'*.

French was born on 1st May 1845 at Cloonyquin, County Roscommon, the third of nine children, and the second son, to Christopher French, Justice of the Peace and High Sheriff of Roscommon, and his wife, Susan nee Percy. His was a privileged, sheltered childhood, cocooned in the wealth and easy life of the Big House, the Landed Gentry, or as he himself later humourously dubbed them, the *'Stranded Gentry'*.

In 1872 he entered Trinity College, Dublin to study engineering, fulfilling his father's hopes and aspirations for him. During his time there, he made a name for himself entertaining with music and song, accompanied by his banjo, an instrument which had become very fashionable in society. It was at this time that the Gaiety Theatre was opened, with French a frequent attender, because, as he himself wrote: *'Music held me with its magic spell.'*

In 1883 the Irish Board of Works appointed French as Inspector of Loans to Tenants, under a government drainage scheme for County Cavan, so he became known as Inspector of Drains in Cavan. This ended in September 1888.

Thereafter he became involved in writing for the 'Jarvey', a magazine which allowed him free rein for his humour, satire and anecdote. However, due to financial difficulties, the last issue of the 'Jarvey' was Christmas 1890, just two years later. He also wrote for *'The Irish Cyclist and Athlete Magazine'*.

In June 1890, he married Ethel Armytage-Moore, daughter of Hugh Armytage, land agent for Lord Farnham. Ettie, as she was known, was a talented artist, and he referred to her as his *'Ray of Sunshine'*. Sadly, just after a year and a day of marriage, Ettie died in childbirth, from septicaemia, and their baby daughter followed her just a few weeks later.

The death of his beloved Ettie marked a great water-shed in his life. The once happy-go-lucky French changed, now adopting a much more serious attitude to life and a much more professional attitude to developing his career in the entertainment world through comic opera, composing music with Dr. Collison, with whom he formed a life-time partnership. Even his hair changed over a short period of time from brown to white.

However, he did find love again shortly afterwards, with Helen Sheldon, a friend of one of the main members of the cast of French's comic opera 'Strongbow'. Lennie, as she was known, was an accomplished pianist and the couple married in January 1894, when French was 39 and Lennie 25. They enjoyed a long and happy marriage together, Lennie bringing elements of support and stability back into French's life. They lived first in Dublin, where their first two daughters were born, Ethel, named after French's first wife and Mollie, before moving to London where their third daughter, Joan was born.

English society at the beginning of the 20th Century, with its world of private entertaining and the growth of lecture societies, meant that French, with his great versatility as an entertainer, was in great demand. He delighted and charmed with his songs, banjo and painting, including his unique smoke painting, where all he needed was a lighted candle, the back of a plate and a match. His paintings were enhanced no doubt by his ability to see things upside-down, hence his famous paintings of reflections in water.

French died in January 1920, at the home of his cousin, Canon Richardson, in Formby, near Liverpool, where he stopped to rest on his way home from entertaining in Glasgow. He developed pneumonia, and died within a very short period of time just after Lennie arrived to nurse him. He is buried in St. Luke's Churchyard, Formby, Merseyside.

William Percy French is probably best remembered for his melodies, songs and satires. But there was a lot more to him than *'The Mountains of Mourne', 'The Emigrant's Letter',* or even his famous satirical *'Are ye right there Michael', 'Phil the Fluter's Ball',* or *'Slattery's Mounted Fut'*.

Just as with William Butler Yeats, there was also a deeply Spiritual side to William Percy French. Spirituality transcends religion. William Percy French transcended religion. As we saw earlier, Spirituality is all about connecting with what lies beyond our five physical human senses. It is a desire, a longing, a search to find and to appreciate more than we can see and hear in what we consider to be our natural reality.

Music can best be described as a **'vibrational gateway',** that gateway admitting us into the higher vibrational frequency energy levels which surround us constantly on all sides. Music, as we have seen throughout this book, brings us into an expanded state of awareness, an expanded state of consciousness, where we can connect with these other vibrational frequencies that surround us. And when we are in that expanded state of awareness, that is when we experience that loving, harmonious state of feeling for which we all yearn.

William Percy French, like all our literary and musical greats, acknowledged these higher vibrational frequency levels, the presence of other forms of life and energy around us. A consciousness that is in all living things and moves through all things. Call them the fairy folk, the little folk, whatever, but they are there in our waters, our forests, our flowers, our vegetation, our soil, our mountains. Our ancestors acknowledged them, and respected them, as do the peoples of Eastern countries and Eastern religions.

'The hills are alive with the sound of music' suddenly takes on a whole new meaning when we acknowledge these other forms of life around us, all vibrating on different energy frequency levels from our own. Just like the wave frequencies on a radio, or on a television, they are there, all around us, we are just not tuned into them.

And William Percy French certainly acknowledged them! And having three young daughters, who needed to be entertained, would certainly have helped him to move in and out of various levels of consciousness very easily, between the fairy worlds, those worlds of the nature spirits, on the one hand, and the human world on the other.

In *'Innismeela'*, we have all the words. All the words associated with the worlds of the little folk: *'Fairy ring.....Fairy Man.... Queen of Fairyland....the little people......moonbeams.'* And French associated all these with a *'Celestrial Stream'* and *'The Golden Light'*.

' I can only see the moonbeams that on Innismeela float,

But if I slept inside the fairies' ring

I could see them sailing, sailing in their little silver boat,

And I'd hear the song the little people sing.

For the Fairy Man has told me how he slumbered there one day,

And woke to find them dancing on the shore,

And still he hears them singing, though 'tis faint and far away

Eileen McCourt

And he's wishing he was with them ever more.

I've seen the Queen of Fairyland! I've heard her wondrous song

With her to heights of happiness I have flown,

Now I know the days are weary, now I know the nights are long,

For the one I love has left me all alone.

Innismeela! Innismeela! There's a sleep that knows no dream,

And its in that dreamless slumber I shall be,

For I know that I shall waken by some still celestial stream

And through the golden light come to me'.

In '*A Fairy Song*' we again have all the words running through: '*Fairies..... Fairyland...... Elfin Band... Moonbeams...Glow-worms*'.

Stay, silver ray,

Till the airy way we wing

To the shade of the glade

Where the fairies dance and sing:

The mortals are asleep -

They can never understand

That night brings delight,

It Is day in Fairyland

Music of the Spheres

Float, golden note,

From the lute strings all in tune,

Climb, quiv'ring chime,

Up the moonbeams to the moon.

There is music on the river,

There is music on the strand,

Night brings delight,

It is day in Fairyland.

Sing while we swing

From the bluebell's lofty crest.

Hey! Come and play,

Sleepy songbirds in your nest;

The glow-worm lamps are lit,

Come and join our Elfin band,

Night brings delight,

It is day in Fairyland.

Roam thro' the home

Eileen McCourt

Where the little children sleep,

Light in our flight

Where the curly ringlets peep.

Some shining eyes may see us,

But the babies understand,

Night brings delight,

It is day in Fairyland.'

At some stage in our lives, for each of us, there comes a wake-up call. Some particular event or happening which causes us to question, which triggers something in the depths of our being, to remember the reason for our existence here on Planet Earth and the whole meaning behind life and creation. Some event or happening which makes us realise and accept that we are part of a bigger picture, a microcosm of the macrocosm that is all of the vastness of entire creation. Some event or happening which makes us consider our own physical mortality, and what lies beyond our physical existence.

William Percy French questioned all this in his explicitly named poem *'Here and Hereafter'*.

Music of the Spheres

'The wide wide sea

Is a joy to see

I stand by that heaving plain,

And feast mine eyes

On the sunset skies

And the distant mountain chain.

It make one think

How the hills will shrink

And the ocean seem a pond,

When we stand by the sea

Of Eternity,

And wonder what lies beyond.'

For William Percy French, that wake-up call came with the tragic death of his first wife, Ettie, who died of septicaemia in childbirth at the tender age of just eighteen, and their baby daughter followed her just a few weeks later. Her tragic death and his great personal loss made him question deeply his own understanding of human existence, and his own significance in the greater scheme of things.

In *'Not lost but gone before'*, we can clearly see how William Perch

Eileen McCourt

French considered physical death to be just that, a physical ending only. He knows that he and Ettie will meet again!

'Once, only once, upon a time,

We heard the bells of faerie chime,

And through the golden nights and days

They sang their Elfin roundelays.

The world and we were in our prime

Once, only once, upon a time.

Has Fairyland for ever flown?

– The darkness falls on me alone,

For on my sweet companion's eyes

There shines the light of Paradise.

The heights of joy I cannot climb

As we did once upon a time.

Oh, loved one of the far away,

I know that we shall meet some day,

Music of the Spheres

And once again walk hand in hand

Through all the realms of Fairyland.

And Heaven's own harps around us chime,

As they did – once upon a time!'

And as he looked at his young wife lying dead:

'Only goodnight sweetheart,

And not farewell,

Though for all times thou art

Where angels dwell.

Though for a time those eyes

Lose their soft light,

Let there be no good-byes,

Only goodnight.

Though for a time they toll

Thy passing bell,

Eileen McCourt

'Tis but goodnight, sweet soul,

And not farewell.

O'er thy sweet lips I sigh -

Lips cold and white,

There! - that is not good-bye.

Only goodnight'.

The headstone on Ettie's grave, in Mount Jerome Cemetery, reads:

'Ettie, the beloved wife of W. Percy French, who died June 29th 1891'.

Followed by:

'Rest - sleep came early, better so,

Since waking means but weeping;

And we who still the struggle know,

Half envy thee thy sleeping.

Rest - never to the silent sod,

A kindlier heart was given;

Music of the Spheres

No purer soul returns to God

No sweeter life to Heaven.'

One of French's most famous and best known poems is '*Gortnamona*', one of what he called his '*pathetic poems*', also written after Ettie's death. There certainly is a great deal of pathos in it. We have the analogy of raindrops for tears, the birds singing, the wind sighing, the banshee crying, and his loved one, Ettie, not dead, but just '*sleeping*'.

'Long, long ago in the woods of Gortnamona,

I thought the birds were singing in the blackthorn tree;

But oh, it was my heart that was ringing, ringing, ringing,

With the joy that you were bringing, oh my love, to me.

Long, long ago in the woods of Gortnamona,

I thought the wind was sighing round the blackthorn tree;

But oh, it was the banshee that was crying, crying, crying,

And I knew my love was dying far across the sea.

Now if you go through the woods of Gortnamona,

You hear the raindrops creeping through the blackthorn tree;

But oh, it is the tears I am weeping, weeping, weeping,

For the loved one that is sleeping far away from me. '

After Ettie's tragic death, William Percy French went to Wales, taking with him his bicycle, and spent a year painting in the quiet, in the peace and in the tranquillity in which he immersed himself. His paintings exhibited the realisation on his part that there was a world outside his own world of reason and the five physical senses, a far greater and much deeper reality. Light became central to his paintings and his water colourings. Light was a spiritual thing for French. His unique technique with Light on the horizon, Light emanating through cloudy skies onto bog and moor, Light shimmering through the flowing and moving waters, Light oozing into dark landscapes, all reflected his own deeply spiritual belief in Light being the manifestation, the emanation, the creating power of God in evidence. He had indeed called Ettie his '*Ray of Sunshine*'. She was the Light in his life.

So it is noteworthy that at his funeral he had arranged for the hymn '*Lead Kindly Light*' to be played.

Music of the Spheres

'Lead, kindly Light, amid th'encircling gloom, lead Thou me on!

The night is dark, and I am far from home; lead Thou me on!

    Keep Thou my feet; I do not ask to see

    The distant scene; one step enough for me.

I was not ever thus, nor prayed that Thou shouldst lead me on;

I loved to choose and see my path; but now lead Thou me on!

    I loved the garish day, and, spite of fears,

    Pride ruled my will. Remember not past years!

So long Thy power hath blest me, sure it still will lead me on.

O'er moor and fen, o'er crag and torrent, till the night is gone,

    And with the morn those angel faces smile, which I

    Have loved long since, and lost awhile!

Meantime, along the narrow rugged path, Thyself hast trod,

Lead, Savior, lead me home in childlike faith, home to my God.

    To rest forever after earthly strife

    In the calm light of everlasting life.'

Yes, William Percy French was deeply spiritually connected. Connected to the Great Universal Consciousness, to All That Is. And connected to the other energy vibrational frequencies that he knew surrounded him. Connected too to the whole understanding of energy, we ourselves being energy and therefore we cannot ever end, we will never die.

And in listening to the music of William Percy French, brought to us by Irish composer pianist Pat McCourt, where Pat has also composed the music to accompany some of French's poetry, we too can reach the *'heights of joy'* that can only be reached when we are in an expanded state of consciousness, and William Percy French and Pat McCourt are our gateway into that heightened vibrational energy level.

Conclusion

"If Music be the food of love, play on!"

Music plays an important part in Shakespeare's dramas, and is often used to carry the plot. The words of Duke Orsino of Illyria, taken from Shakespeare's *'Twelfth Night'* show that the Duke sees the cure for his unrequited love for Countess Olivia as being a surfeit of music:

'If music be the food of love, play on, / Give me excess of it; that surfeiting, / The appetite may sicken and so die.'

The Great Universal Energy, that which we call God, is everything. God is indeed synonymous with Love, and so Love is everything. Love is all there is. So if music is the food of Love, then music is the nourisher of all that is.

We have seen throughout this book that everything, including ourselves is energy, and energy is simply vibrational frequencies. The only difference in any form of energy is the frequency on which it is vibrating.

We have seen too, that we are surrounded constantly on all sides by higher vibrational energy frequencies, interconnecting and communicating with us at all times.

Music is the *'vibrational gateway'* for us into these higher frequencies, as it brings us into expanded states of spiritual awareness, without which we cannot access these higher states.

We are able, through the music, to make an increased connection with our own Higher Self, which is us in our natural inherent pure God Essence, our own unique divine spark. When we listen to music that resonates with our being, we are feeling high-frequency emotions of unconditional love, a profound sense of peace and happiness, even ecstasy, and a deep connection to the Great Universal God Consciousness, to All That Is. We are experiencing a profound sense of belonging, because we are all One in this Great Universal God Energy.

Everything, as we also have seen, emits a sound that goes out from us into the ether, joining the Great Universal Energy Stream, and as there are no straight lines in the entirety of all Creation, everything that we send out comes back to us. That is the irrefutable law of the Universe. It just cannot be otherwise and there are no exceptions whatsoever to this rule.

The Symphony of Life! The great cosmic orchestral harmony! The musical harmony that resonates throughout all of creation, the Music of the Spheres!

Einstein said that the most amazing and fascinating thing about our universe is that it is comprehensible. This was a follow-on from Pythagoras himself over 2500 years ago teaching that the universe is rational and structured. There is a unity to all things, with mathematics and numbers holding everything together in the One Great Universal Energy, teaching us the truth about nature and the cosmos.

How often do we use the phrase *'getting tuned in'*? Constantly! We just do not use it in terms of getting our musical instruments *'tuned in'* or getting our singing voices *'tuned in'*, but we use it in terms of getting ourselves *'tuned in'*. And by that we mean getting ourselves connected to our own Higher Self, to the Great God Consciousness, to enable us to *'go with the flow'* instead of pushing against it.

The sonar calls of the whales and the dolphins, the birdsong, the whisper of the wind, the rustle of the leaves, the gushing of our streams and rivers, the crashing of the waves on our shores, - all melodies created in the Great Universal Cosmic Orchestra, the musical harmony that binds us all together, the harmony for which our soul yearns and thirsts to be a part of, and not apart from.

And why? Simply because that harmonious vibrational frequency, that harmonious dimension for which our soul thirsts, is where we have all come from, and to where we are all destined to eventually return. And we can experience that harmonious joy and happiness while still on this dense lower vibrational frequency earth plane.

Yes, we can experience it through our great musical composers.

As the music flows through them, they are in an expanded state of awareness, an expanded state of consciousness, where they are feeling spiritual emotions, where they *become* the music, where they *are* the music.

When McCourt plays, he hears nothing around him, he is cut off from all immediate interference or distractions. He exists in a bubble, just himself and the music. He cannot communicate with anyone around him. That's because he is on a higher vibrational frequency. And that's because music is not just affecting his aural senses, but also his visual sensory mechanisms. Yes! Music is visual as well as aural! How often have you been driving along in traffic or looking for a particular address, and you turn the music down? Ever wondered why you do this? Simply because your vision is involved with the music, you are seeing it as well as hearing it.

McCourt has produced numerous CDs, and just lately, two DVDs. He has put to music several of the works of William Percy French and William Butler Yeats, who are undoubtedly two of Ireland's literary greats.

In the DVDs, McCourt has synchronised spiritual visuals with the spirituality of music. The divine thought forms triggered in the viewer through the spectacular scenery in Ireland associated with French and Yeats, combined simultaneously with the melodies, harmonious to the ear, becomes a catalyst for the listener, propelling him into states of truly expanded consciousness.

As McCourt captures the mood of each melody, he moves beyond his physical consciousness, taking us with him. He is the bridge for us between the world of matter and physicality and the ethereal world, connecting us from our earthly plane consciousness frequency vibrational level to an expanded consciousness level, for which we all yearn.

McCourt has composed music for the works of Yeats, including:

Music of the Spheres

' In memory of Eva Gore-Booth and Con Markievicz'

'Under Bare Ben Bulben's Head'

The Wild Swans at Coole'

'The Stolen Child'

'Lake Isle of Innisfree'

and for William Percy French:

'Not lost but gone before'

'Only goodnight'

'A Fairy Song'

'To the West'

'Here and Hereafter'

'Epitaph on Ettie's gravestone'

McCourt's music, like all music that resonates with our very being, is indeed a catalyst to remind us of our inherent connection to a greater reality, a larger reality of worlds that can only be felt or sensed, but not seen with our limited human vision. His music helps and enables us to rise above our daily grind and expand our consciousness to acknowledge and embrace a much greater perspective, allowing us to tap into other realms via the different frequency levels and the subtle, but non-invasive energy fields that exist all around us.

With McCourt, we can indeed join with and experience the Music of the Spheres!

Other Books by Eileen McCourt

Eileen has written thirteen other books, all of which are available on Amazon as either print copies or Kindle. For more information, visit her author page: www.eileenmccourt.co.uk

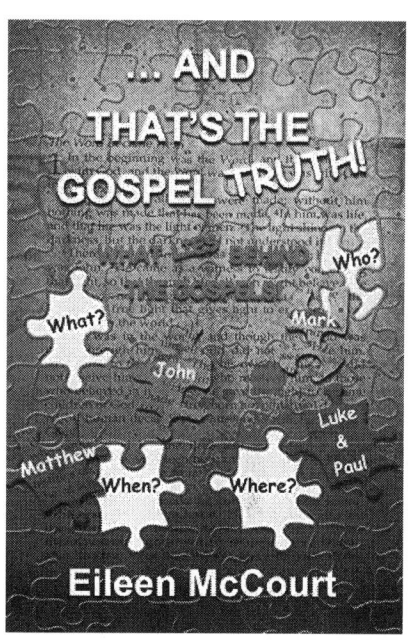

Printed in Poland
by Amazon Fulfillment
Poland Sp. z o.o., Wrocław